Appointment in Japan

一英国人教師のみた日本

回顧六十年

G.C.アレン

George Allen, on his arrival in Nagoya, 1922

Appointment in Japan
Memories of Sixty Years

G. C. Allen

THE ATHLONE PRESS
London

First published 1983 by The Athlone Press Ltd
58 Russell Square, London WC1B 4HL

© Estate of G. C. Allen, 1983

Distributor in the USA and Canada
Humanities Press Inc
New Jersey

British Library Cataloguing in Publication Data
Allen, G. C.
Appointment in Japan.
1. Japan – History
I. Title
952.03   DS881
ISBN 0-485-11237-X

All rights reserved. No part of this publication may be reproduced, stored in a retrieval system, or transmitted in any form or by any means, electronic, mechanical, photocopying or otherwise, without prior permission in writing from the publisher.

Printed in Great Britain by
Nene Litho, Earls Barton, Northants

Bound by Woolnough Bookbinding,
Wellingborough, Northants

Contents

	Publisher's Note	viii
	List of Illustrations	ix
I	Arrival at the City of Fame and Antiquity	1
II	A Bachelor's Household in Nagoya	16
III	Town and Country in the 1920s	34
IV	Students and Teachers	57
V	How Others See Us	78
VI	Manner, Moods and Convictions	99
VII	Disaster and Discord	120
VIII	Recreations, Travels and Encounters	137
IX	Economic Progress and Social Development	158
X	*Dai Nihon* and Great Britain	175
	Glossary	191
	Index	195

IN PRIVATE LIFE, COURTEOUS, IN PUBLIC LIFE, DILIGENT,
IN RELATIONSHIPS, LOYAL.

The Analects of Confucius
in the translation by A. Waley

Publisher's Note

We are fortunate that Professor Allen completed his revision of the manuscript shortly before his death.

We have to thank his executors for their help in obtaining the manuscript, in particular Professor Margaret Gowing of the University of Oxford, who ensured that all the papers were made available. Thanks are also due to Nagoya University, The Japan Foundation and Mr Isamu Takashima for assistance in locating photographs.

We have also to acknowledge the help of Professor Allen's friends in the Kitankai (the alumni association of Nagoya University), in particular the assistance of Mr Isamu Takashima and Mr S. Takayama, whose support made possible the publication of this book.

Illustrations

George Allen, 1922 *frontispiece*

between pages 118–9
George Allen, 1979
Welcome party for George Allen, Tokyo, 1979
Welcome party for George Allen, Nagoya, 1979
The Japan Foundation Award Ceremony, 1980

I

Arrival at the City of Fame and Antiquity

In the early years of the present century, W. J. Ashley, whose reputation until then had been based on his distinction as Mediaeval Economic Historian, set out on his career as a pioneer of higher business education in Britain. For the next twenty-five years he presided over the Faculty of Commerce at the University of Birmingham. It is symptomatic of national attitudes towards innovation that, while British firms regarded the venture with coolness, if not suspicion, the Mitsui family of Japan, which for centuries had been prominent in Japanese commerce and finance, should send one of its members to become an early pupil. The Japanese at that time were no strangers to higher business education. The precursor of what was afterwards the Tokyo University of Commerce (Shodai) and today is Hitotsubashi University, was founded in the 1870s. As always, they were eager to discover what others had to teach them.

The connection with Birmingham, once established, persisted. From the 1900s on the Japanese government founded a number of *Koto Shogyo Gakko* (Commercial High Schools), modelled on the German Handelshochschulen, and each of the schools recruited several foreigners to their staff. On frequent occasions, when they wanted an English lecturer, the authorities asked Ashley to recommend candidates for the post, and several Birmingham men were chosen during the next twenty-five years to fill these vacancies. In the spring of 1922, Ashley was asked to recommend someone for a lectureship at a *Koto Shogyo Gakko* that had been opened at Nagoya, in Central Japan, during the previous year. Ashley was then tutoring me in my post-graduate year at Birmingham, and he asked me if I would like the job, a two-year appointment. I was somewhat taken aback by his suggestion, since I had other plans in mind. But he strongly urged me to allow my name to be put forward as a candidate. "You will have a splendid opportunity of seeing the world at other people's expense and the privilege of living for some years in a civilisation very different from our own." It did not take long to decide, and I remember that the confirmation of the appointment was brought to me in June 1922, just as I was about to enter the University Hall for an examination. By this time I was eagerly looking forward to the adventure, and so the news did not put me off my stride. I was then almost twenty-two years of age.

Less than two months later I found myself on board the *Suwa Maru*, a 10,000 ton passenger-cargo liner of the Nippon Yusen Kaisha fleet. For seven weeks I revelled in the sights, sounds and smells of the ports – Marseilles, Port Said, Aden, Bombay, Colombo, Singapore, Hong Kong and Shanghai – before arriving at Kobe in the middle of September. The passengers on the ship were as varied in nationality as in calling – British, American, German, Dutch, Swiss, Scandinavian, Chinese and, of course, Japanese. Many of them were old China hands on the way back to Shanghai to resume their business activities. Others were officially returning from leave and there were the few academics. I enjoyed the stimulating company. The old China hands were intent on instructing me, or disillusioning me, about the ways of the East, and a pleasantly satirical Chinese pulled my leg about the part I was going to play in sustaining the White Man's Burden! The Japanese held themselves rather aloof from the rest of the company, although I found that they had not been slow in speculating among themselves about the status and charac-

Arrival at the City

ter of the various Westerners. When they heard that I was going to teach in Japan, some of them took me in hand and tried to explain to me the things in their country that I was likely to consider strange. So far as I was concerned, I hinted, the stranger the better. I was amused when a kindly academic, who evidently assumed that I was probably equipped with all the prejudices of the typical Englishman in foreign parts, went out of his way to convince me, as we sailed from port to port, of the common humanity of the Indian peddler, the Malay docker, the Chinese rickshaw coolie and the English schoolmaster. The most distinguished scholar on board was Professor Inouye, an elderly philosopher. One day I was admitted to his presence and honoured by an introduction to him. After initial courtesies he announced, to my discomfiture: "I am a Hegelian philosopher." I fear that he was disappointed in me for I could not then declare, nor could I have subsequently declared, a commitment to any system of philosophic principles.

These shipboard excitements at last came to an end one morning in the middle of September when I disembarked at Kobe, eager for new experiences. By the afternoon of that day I found myself travelling by train to Nagoya where I was to make my home. The weather was warm and an unfamiliar landscape unfolded before me in the sunshine. Through the carriage window I looked out on terraced rice fields and tea plantations. Rising steeply in the background were forest-clad hills. Here and there, on slight eminences above the cultivated plain, half-hidden in clusters of pine trees, were temples and shrines. In the fields men and women, dressed in white and blue costumes of unfamiliar style, with their heads protected by wide straw hats, were harvesting, or trudging along narrow tracks beside small heavily-laden carts pulled by oxen, horses or straining dogs. When the train passed through towns and villages I caught brief glimpses of streets, or groups of unpainted wooden houses, roofed with heavy blue-grey tiles or deep thatch. Occasionally a modern factory, built incongruously of concrete, came into view, the only type of building in the landscape that recalled the Western world. The advertisements displayed along some stretches of the line were fascinating. Since I could not read the characters in which they were written, I remained ignorant of their banality.

    The excitement roused by the strange scene was no less than that I felt when I turned my eyes on the interior of the railway carriage. It was a single compartment with a long, blue, velvet-covered seat on each side. Most of the passengers had either removed their outer garments altogether or had drawn them about their knees and were sitting at ease on their heels, leaving their footgear on the floor in front of them. From time to time they fanned themselves, opening their dress to give access to the cooling air. Using towels, a few had tied small blocks of ice to the top of their heads, a form of refrigeration which obviously enabled them to endure the heat of the afternoon without discomfort. In the luggage racks were bundles of varying size held together by squares of cloth tied at the corners. These, as I was soon to find out, were called *furoshiki*, a most convenient and flexible means of carrying one's possessions. Only a small minority of the men were dressed in Western style, even if those who had removed their coats and trousers were included. All the women were dressed in *kimono*. I was an intruder from another world.

    Whenever the train halted at a station, through the windows vendors handed earthenware tea-pots containing green tea, and handleless cups, or neat wooden boxes containing cold rice and pickles, or little string bags of fruit. A few children, more gaily dressed than their elders, ran uninhibitedly up and down the carriage. Some of them stopped and stared at me, but fled in terror if I seemed to take notice of them. When they did so their parents smiled and gave me friendly nods in order to dispel any embarrassment that this might cause me.

    It was a doubly distracting journey. I was reluctant to miss any scene in the passing countryside, but once my eyes had turned to the charms of the carriage it was an effort to

Arrival at the City

withdraw them. The conversation of the passengers flowed over me, ceaseless and uncomprehended, yet I was content to think that, later on, these sounds might perhaps convey something to me.

In the late afternoon the conductor appeared at the door of the carriage, doffed his peaked cap, bowed and informed us that we were approaching Nagoya station. He appealed to us politely not to leave anything behind. Of course, I could not understand what he said at the time; but I found afterwards that he was making the conventional speech on the approach to a station. This is almost the only feature of a Japanese railway journey that has remained unchanged during the last sixty years. Nowadays the passengers are provided with pullman seats and the carriages on the main line trains are air-conditioned. Most passengers wear Western-style suits and dresses and their picturesque and informal travelling habits have been discarded. The landscape as seen from the main Tokaido line is no longer one of terraced rice fields and thatched farmhouses. Although these remain, they are being submerged by a swelling wave of factories, tall blocks of flats and offices, concrete elevated roads and new tracks and bridges for the high-speed trains. Farming has become highly mechanised and the fields are sparsely peopled.

My recollection of the actual arrival is vague. I recall a confused group of railway officials and colleagues-to-be all trying to help me to gather my luggage and set me on my way to a hotel. There were then no taxis in Nagoya. My luggage travelled in a handcart and I myself was installed in a rickshaw. Before setting off I was guilty of the first of my long series of social solecisms. I tried to tip a helpful policeman under the impression that he was a railway official. My offering was brushed aside. This mistake was my first introduction to two important features of Japanese society. One was that Japan was one country in the world where tips were not only not expected but were actually refused. The other was that the police of that period, though inclined to be busy-bodies and sometimes overbearing and harsh, had too much pride to accept presents, in spite of their poverty.

As I left the station, I had my first glimpse of the town that was to be my home. I confess to having felt some disappointment. At close quarters the low, unpainted buildings (with single or double storeys) looked drab. The streets were untidy, dusty and rough of surface. Single-decker tramcars screeched as they took the curves on their uneven tracks and a confusion of wires and cables hung from the corners of buildings and from apparently toppling poles. Yet, in contrast, there were the crowds going about their business, half-naked peasants with ox-carts, coolies in blue tunics which bore characters designating the name of their employer, solid citizens in sombre and dignified *kimono*, the women with elaborate coiffures and the brightly clad children. I heard for the first time the clatter of *geta* (wooden clogs) on the footpaths.

In the 1920s, visitors who required foreign-style rooms had no choice but to stay at the Nagoya Hotel, an old wooden structure of a kind favoured by architects of Western-style buildings in the *Meiji* period (1868–1912). It had a Japanese section which looked attractive, but for the rest it was rather bleak and not very comfortable. The rooms were sometimes invaded by rats, and I heard that one of the guests who stayed there for some months had amused himself by shooting them with a revolver as he lay in bed. I myself, being preoccupied with all my new experiences, was not in a mood to be critical of the accommodation and I settled in contentedly for a few nights. Presently, A. E. Nicholls, an English fellow-lecturer at the College, called to take me out to dinner.

By this time the sun had set, and when we left the hotel the scene had been transformed. The drabness was gone. I was conscious now only of bright colour and movement. The *shoji* (sliding paper screens) were drawn back from the rooms which fronted the streets and the brilliantly lit interiors of restaurants, shops, workplaces and dwellings were exposed to view. Cyclists carrying Japanese lanterns

Arrival at the City

wove their way skilfully among the pedestrians. By now the inhabitants of Nagoya were emerging from the bath houses and had dressed themselves in light-coloured cotton *yukata* (unlined summer *kimono*) for their evening stroll. The contrast between the dull day-time appearance of a Japanese town and its brightness and gaiety after sunset made an immediate impact, and was a recurrent pleasure in the years to come.

My colleague took me into one of the few restaurants in Nagoya which then served European, or rather pseudo-European, food. I already knew that Japanese domestic habits were peculiar: for instance, that people normally squatted on the floor and removed their footgear before entering a room in the interests of cleanliness. I now found that, in buildings of a Western type, a compromise was permitted. As we entered the restaurant, a servant fitted our shoes with cloth covers. We mounted a narrow, rickety staircase to a small room furnished in the yellowish, highly polished, deal tables and chairs that I was later to find in many foreign-style restaurants. The room was at least bright and cheerful and the *kimono* of the waitresses gay and colourful. I have no recollection of the meal, though I am sure that it carried the flavours that invariably characterised Japanese versions of Western food. I felt frustrated at being unable to join in the conversation with the other guests and the waitresses, except tediously through the medium of my friend who acted as interpreter. This was the only blemish on my first evening in Japan.

The next morning my first call was to the Mitsui Bank where I went to open an account. The hotel provided me with a rickshaw and I was set down at a solid stone building with Corinthian pillars and marble floors which seemed an arrogant intruder among the modest wooden structures adjacent to it. It was then one of the dominating presences in the main street of Nagoya where tall modern buildings in brick or concrete were still exceptional – outside the centre of the town such buildings were hardly to be found at all. They housed banks, department stores (known as *departo*), public offices and insurance companies. When a year or two later the American YMCA put up a small block of flats for its members, it was a pioneer in providing residential accommodation of this kind.

The Mitsui Bank was one of the few buildings in Nagoya to survive the bombing of the city during the Second World War. A few years ago, I looked out from a top window of the new, massive Tokai Bank and saw far below, dwarfed by its lofty neighbours, the old once-impressive bank building where I had opened my account almost sixty years previously. The process of opening the account was quite lengthy for the local branch had few foreign clients. I had not yet realised that a cheque currency was not highly developed in Japan and the bank seemed disinclined to allow me the current account which I had requested. Yet they attended to me with ceremony, handed me cups of green tea, and finally acquiesced. After everything was completed I was bowed out with much politeness.

While I was conducting my business I observed for the first time the operation of the *soroban* or abacus. Every clerk, I noted, was equipped with one of these useful instruments. I afterwards found that its use was taught systematically in the schools. It was indispensable for all arithmetical calculations by shopkeepers, clerks and others engaged in business transactions. Even the simplest calculation called for the *soroban*. Reliance on it, so it was said, made the Japanese weak in mental arithmetic. However, it had many advantages and enabled calculations to be checked and re-checked very easily. Whenever one entered a bank or other kind of office, one was sure to hear a clerk calling out figures for addition. Each figure was followed by the rapid click of the beads.

Later that day I was summoned to meet the Principal of the College to which I had been appointed. My introduction was effected with some formality. A Japanese professor of English arrived at the hotel in one of the few motor cars then to be seen in Nagoya and I was taken through the city to the College which was on the southern outskirts. Here I

Arrival at the City

was introduced to my future colleagues, shown round the lecture rooms and library and welcomed amiably by the Principal, Dr R. Watanabe. He was very considerate and was kind enough to allow me a fortnight or so in which to get used to my new environment and to find suitable accommodation.

I cannot remember that he gave me any kind of advice, except to stress that it was important that I should please the students. This is a point to which I shall return; at the time, his hint amused me. I was then only twenty-two and I am sure that I must have appeared excessively young and brash to some of my colleagues, including English, German and Canadian teachers then in their forties. I was, however, never made to feel uncomfortable for that reason, not even by the students, some of whom were almost my own age. Despite their reverence for their elders, in making appointments, the Japanese have never been put off by a candidate's lack of years, provided that they are confident that he is competent. Towards the end of my stay, when I was helping to find someone to fill the vacancy caused by my intended departure, the Principal said to me: "Send us someone with ability." He added significantly: "As you know, we do not mind how young he is." So, here I was, installed as a *sensei* (teacher) and designated in English as "Professor". After a few weeks I ceased to feel a fool when so addressed.

I made good use of my fortnight's grace. I explored the highways and byways of Nagoya. I paid a brief visit to Kyoto where I stayed for the first time in a Japanese inn. I fell in love with Kyoto and never missed a chance to revisit it. I then had only a few words of Japanese, but I set out every day with map and guide-book in search of the exquisite treasures which abound. When I got lost, as often happened, I called a rickshaw and was taken back to my starting point. I also spent some part of my first weeks in Japan in learning the spoken language. I started with a child's grammar book. The lady who taught me had her own methods. She spoke a sentence in Japanese. Then she held up her hands and said in English: "I have ten toes" – *yubi* being the same word for fingers and toes. I still found time to prepare what I hoped would be suitable lectures.

A Canadian missionary sufficiently overcame his prejudice against Englishmen to invite me to stay with him until I had found permanent quarters. As he had a long experience of Japan, he taught me a good deal about the problems of living in that country, even though some of his opinions of Japanese ways naturally reflected the bias of his calling. He spent a great deal of effort in raising money from the rich for his philanthropic ventures. He could never understand why anyone with money to spare should spend it in buying a scroll painting or what he called an "old bowl" when it might have gone to the provision of quarters for the YMCA.

Nowadays the Japanese make life easy for foreign visitors by giving the names of railway stations and some streets and premises in *romaji* (Roman letters) as well as in Chinese characters, or in one of their own syllabaries (lists of letters based on phonetic sounds). When I arrived in Japan, however, only the main stations could be identified by the foreigner and the use of *romaji* was very limited. Thus I found myself in a world where I could not read the public communications, the names of premises or the content of advertisements. In trying to grapple with the consequent problems I came to realise that the Chinese characters often gave rise to serious difficulties for the Japanese themselves. I found that it was advisable to send telegrams in *katakana* (one of the two Japanese syllabaries) and to inscribe the envelopes of letters in *kanji* (Chinese characters) as well as in *romaji* in order to ensure a reasonably quick delivery. For inscriptions in Chinese characters I had to seek the help of Japanese colleagues.

Soon after I arrived I had to write to a well-known Bank of Japan official to whom I had a letter of introduction. His surname was Ko and a colleague, on being asked to write this name for me in *kanji*, demurred. "Which Ko is it?" he asked, "there are many ways of writing it." In other words,

Arrival at the City

until he had seen how Ko was written he could not write it himself. On subsequent occasions I observed that my colleagues often argued with each other when I asked them to write an unfamiliar address for me.

There is much beauty in the Chinese characters which are an integral part of Japanese art. But their use for everyday communication must have been a serious hindrance to the Japanese in their efforts to adapt themselves to the modern world. My German colleague, a philologist, and a keen student of the Japanese language, was openly contemptuous of *kanji* as a means of written communication. In frivolous moments I was inclined to think that the Japanese were content to accept this handicap because they were so conscious of their superiority over other peoples. The race would have been unfair to other competitors if they had not carried this self-imposed weight! However, I am told that the Chinese characters offer some advantages in scientific exposition. Since it is possible to invent (by combination) entirely new characters to express clearly defined scientific relations or terms, there may be a gain in precision, for exposition is not confused by using words that have both popular and scientific meanings. In spite of this, it must be confessed that the Japanese have taken over a vast number of English and other foreign terms which they spell out in their syllabaries. In some books on economics, for instance, such terms are found on every other line.

In my life in a city where there were few foreign residents and where only a small proportion of even the academic and business communities spoke English well, I had to come to terms with the language problem early in my career. I found it easy enough to acquire a sufficiency of colloquial Japanese for the ordinary business of living, but my acquaintance with the characters remained rudimentary. The Japanese for their part found English a difficult language to speak and, although there were a few admirable linguists among my colleagues and friends, they were the exception. From Basil Chamberlain (author of *Things Japanese* and many other books on Japan and the

Appointment in Japan

Japanese language) onwards, foreigners have derived a good deal of amusement from Japanese English. I remember with particular pleasure the label on a bottle of Japanese Scotch whisky. It showed a picture of our Houses of Parliament under which was printed: "As drunk only in the House of the Lord".

Sometimes foreign words cannot be expressed easily by the syllabaries, since there are no exact equivalents for the foreign letters or syllables. I had an illustration of this difficulty soon after I took up my appointment. Some of my students had been to see an American film, and the romantic theme inspired one of them the following morning to chalk on the blackboard "Rub is Vest". It took me some time to gather that he had gloriously confused *r* with *l* and *b* with *v* in his attempt to proclaim "Love is Best".

What impressed me most forcibly, however, was not the comic side of Japanese English, but the lyrical expressions which occasionally resulted from the literal translation of Japanese idioms or sentences. I still treasure a letter which I received soon after my coming to Japan from a Japanese with whom I had been friendly in my student days. He had received news of my coming and had speculated about the reasons for it. When I wrote to tell him what I was going to do he replied thus:

> At the first time when I heard of your coming here I played idle game of guess upon it daily. Now, through your letter, it was all clear, but I have to laugh over the distance that my wandering thought has travelled from the truth.

Some time afterwards, one of my Nagoya students, a rather hard-boiled and sophisticated young man, wrote the following note to me as his ship left Yokohama for England:

> The sun dawned brightly, in spite of the wet season, with the twittering of birds, and the day of which I was to set out on my fifty-day long journey to London, leaving my

Arrival at the City

dearest Mother Country, the land of the rising sun and of the perpetual sunshine, came at last.

The claim to perpetual sunshine may be dismissed as poetic licence. Indeed, the writer was describing his mood rather than his objective observation for, in reality, there was little twittering of birds. Quite lately an old student, now a prominent industrialist, accompanied a gift of Japanese tea with a letter which ran:

> The season of fresh verdure has come to Japan and I would like to solicit you to enjoy a smell of light breeze by tasting Japanese green tea. This tea was plucked first in this year and is so-called *shin-cha* (new tea).

The renderings into English of old Japanese or Chinese poems, which friends have sent to me as greetings from time to time, are often felicitous and touching.

I fear that the mistakes which foreigners make in mishandling the Japanese language are ludicrous rather than poetical. I soon found, moreover, that the linguistic difficulties were liable to give rise to serious misunderstandings between Japanese and foreigners. The lack of precision in such communications is attributable in part to the fact that the Japanese language seems to have been devised as a convenient vehicle for those who wish to equivocate. Like any court language it favours ambiguity and offers a way out of any proposition or commitment. The Japanese themselves when they wish to be precise often have to put their point by repetition, using several different turns of speech, and in dealings with foreigners the opportunities for misunderstandings are infinite. In international relations these difficulties show themselves in the drawing up of parallel versions of treaties. To give a simple example, in the Anglo-Japanese Commercial Treaty of 1963, the fact that the Japanese word commonly used as the equivalent of the English term "profession" covers a far wider range of occupations, created drafting problems for the signatories.

Such difficulties arise in all translations of legal docu-

Appointment in Japan

ments, but with Japanese they exist to an extreme degree. Few foreigners are sufficiently well-versed in the language to avoid errors that cause much hilarity among the Japanese. A British diplomat, an excellent linguist, was once conducting some commercial negotiations with Japanese officials. At one stage in the proceedings, when he felt obliged to reject proposals from the other side, he uttered a phrase which was received with amusement. He was puzzled at this reaction until it was pointed out to him that his expression was one used only by women and was often associated with the rejection of amorous advances. This was not an isolated case. Every foreign resident in Japan soon becomes aware of the problems in communication that result from the existence of a hierarchy of synonyms, the use of which depends on the status of the persons engaged in the conversation.

The large number of homonyms in the language cause fewer misunderstandings than might be expected. I suppose that this is because the meaning of a spoken word can generally be inferred from the context or can be made clear in other ways. Sometimes my ignorance of the alternative meanings of words brought surprises. On one occasion I wished to give a present of *nori* (dried seaweed), a delicacy, to a friend and I commissioned someone to buy it for me. I was nonplussed when he returned with a small tube of paste instead of the handsome box or canister that I had expected. I consulted the dictionary and found that *nori*, besides meaning seaweed, also meant paste or starch; it had, indeed, half a dozen other meanings!

Nearly every foreigner, at some stage in his life in Japan, has had the good fortune to find a Japanese friend who will take pains to smooth his path. I myself, along with all the other foreign lecturers at the College, owe a heavy debt to Mr Kenkichi Suzuki, a professor of English who had received much of his education abroad and spoke English fluently. He was, I suppose, deputed by the College authorities to interpret their ways to us and our ways to them. He certainly exerted himself, unobtrusively but

Arrival at the City

tirelessly, to ensure that our life was happy. A senior student, Takeshi Matsumura, also took me under his wing and was of great help in solving the practical problems of living in a novel environment. Ten years later, when I was engaged in research into Japanese industry, he devoted all his free moments to assisting me. When I recall these friends, long dead, I think of the words of Will Adams, the first Englishman in Japan: "The people of this island of Japan are good by nature and courteous above measure." Professor Suzuki and Mr Matsumura both possessed, in addition to these qualities, a keen sense of humour, tolerance and lively intelligence.

II

A Bachelor's Household in Nagoya

The hospitality of the Canadian missionary gave me a chance to look for permanent quarters. As A. E. Nicholls, who had been appointed to the College a year earlier, was also looking for accommodation, we decided to team up and rent a house. Professor Kenkichi Suzuki acted as an intermediary in our negotiations with landlords, and a suitable house was soon found. It was located in a village which, though in the process of becoming a suburb of Nagoya, still retained much of its rural character. It was not a beautiful place, but it was interesting and bordered on the country, within ten minutes' walk of the College. The address, Mizuho-cho, had distinguished historical connotations, for *Mizuho-no-kuni*, "the land of fresh rice ears", was an ancient name for Japan. Our house was situated on a slight eminence, well back from the road, and we had distant views of the agricultural plain that led towards the sea.

It was a typical Japanese dwelling of the old style. Stout wooden uprights rested on large stones sunk in the ground. The roof timbers, fixed by wooden pegs to the uprights, carried a roof of heavy grey tiles. The rooms were floored with *tatami* (reed-covered straw mats) which rested on loose flexible floor-boards laid across the joists, and they were bounded on the two long sides of the house by wide, polished wooden verandahs. The walls on these sides consisted simply of *shoji*, and the other walls were composed of wattle finished on the inside with plaster and sand. The

A Bachelor's Household in Nagoya

wide overhanging eaves protected the interior from sun and rain. At night, and in stormy weather, wooden sliding screens or shutters (*amado*) were drawn into place and the house was then shut up like a box. When this happened, we relied for ventilation on draughts. Since the *amado* did not fit very well we were never in danger of asphyxiation.

The Japanese estimate the size of a house, for the purpose of calculating the rent, according to the number of mats (*tatami*) which it contains. These measure about 6′ × 3′ in area. We had three eight-mat rooms, one of them upstairs (the *nikai*), one six-mat room, a *tatami*-covered *genkan* (entrance hall), two small servants' rooms, a kitchen, a bathroom, two *benjo* (lavatories) and an outhouse.

Two of the rooms possessed a *tokonoma*, a recess supported in one outer corner by a polished wooden pillar, the focal point of a Japanese reception room. Like all Japanese houses, ours was well provided with large cupboards and storage space. It was surrounded by a small garden in which there were maples, clumps of bamboo, pines, flowering cherries and also a prolific medlar tree. Beyond the bamboo hedge which bounded the garden to the north there was a wide area of cultivated farmland.

At that time it was not possible to buy ready-made foreign-style furniture in Nagoya. So my friend and I, with the help of one of our students, induced a local carpenter to construct tables, wicker chairs, bedsteads and the few other articles of furniture which we needed. Cutlery and crockery did not present us with any problems, although we were unable for a long time to find a milk jug. We needed no soft furnishings except cushions. There was no difficulty in getting bed-linen and mattresses, but the only pillows available were the cylindrical hard pillows used by Japanese and just about as comfortable as the good round logs which satisfied our mediaeval ancestors. We were fortunate in being able to borrow down pillows from one of the foreign families in Nagoya.

One of the items of furniture, a tall bookcase, gave rise to some problems. When I came to look for a position for it, I found that it was inclined to topple over when placed on the unstable, *tatami*-covered floors. Finally, I installed it in the *tokonoma* in the best room, which had a firm wooden floor. The *tokonoma* is the focal point of a Japanese room and is usually given over to the display of a scroll painting and an arrangement of flowers. In any gathering the most honoured guest sits nearest to the *tokonoma*. In other words, it is a part of the room which is treated with utmost respect. Many years later I found that my use of the *tokonoma* for housing the bookcase had surprised, if not shocked, some of my visitors. Of course, at the time they concealed their feelings, and I did not become aware of them until a former student told me of the amusement that my solecism had caused.

The house was supplied with no public services except electricity for lighting. It was then the practice for the electricity company to turn on the current at a central switch-board in the evening and to turn it off at dawn. The Japanese normally slept with the light on and thought that foreigners were eccentric in turning off the light when they went to bed. The cables which carried the current to houses in the neighbourhood were festooned on rickety poles and on the corners of buildings. Whenever there was a storm the current failed. Payment for the electricity was related to the number of bulbs in the house; these were replaced free by the electricity company when they were burnt out.

There was no mains drainage in the neighbourhood. Our two cesspools were ladled out periodically by a local farmer to whom our landlord had contracted to sell the contents. We always removed ourselves from the vicinity when this lengthy operation was carried out. Waste water, including water from the bath was carried by a series of little ditches into a village pond which was used for irrigation. The system of surface drainage in the neighbourhood seemed to work very effectively, even in the wettest season. I do not remember whether there was any organised method of rubbish collection. Much of our waste was piled in a heap behind bushes in the garden and from time to time we paid someone to remove it.

A Bachelor's Household in Nagoya

The kitchen was primitive. It was a fairly spacious room with walls of wood and wattle and a beaten earthen floor. In one corner there was a well from which water was pumped, except in hot weather when the well dried up. On the opposite side there was the iron stove for heating the bath water. The fuel used was lignite. The furnishings consisted of a deal table which after a time became mahogany-coloured, and a few shelves. The cooking was done on a clay stove in which the charcoal was brought up to a sufficiently high temperature by fanning it with an *uchiwa*, or round fan. A Western innovation was the tinplate oven which was fitted on the top of the clay stove when our housekeeper ventured to try her hand at a Western recipe. Finally, there was a little shrine before which she placed offerings of rice to keep the kitchen god in good humour.

Our house was considerably larger than those occupied by most of my Japanese colleagues and their families, but we needed more space than they did. The Japanese way of living was economical of space. Every *tatami*-covered room could be used for a diversity of purposes – eating, sleeping and sitting. Furnishings, including the *futon* (mattresses) and bed-linen, could be brought out of the capacious cupboards as they were needed. As soon as Western-style furniture was introduced into a house, rooms became specific to a particular use and more of them were required. Our rent, though reasonable enough, was rather higher than the market rent at that time; the landlord charged us a premium because he doubted whether foreigners were likely to be good tenants. Japanese always remove their shoes or *geta* when they go indoors and put on soft-soled mules. These they leave outside rooms when they enter them. Foreigners had the reputation of disregarding these conventions and of committing other breaches of etiquette.

The old-style Japanese houses were agreeable in the spring and autumn and cool in summer, but they were difficult to heat in winter. As our house was old, the *amado* did not fit and the draughts were biting. We endured the first winter with no heating save that provided by a *hibachi*, a fire-box or large bowl containing small pieces of glowing charcoal bedded in the ashes of burnt straw. Afterwards we obtained our landlord's reluctant consent to use a paraffin oil stove. He was convinced that we would burn down his property, and whenever the local tocsin sounded he came in great haste to see whether his fears were justified. In spite of these anxieties, he refused to insure his property as he grudged paying the premium. We had other evidence of his frugality. One day we found him in the garden cutting a branch from a tree. The wood of this tree was commonly used in the making of *geta* and we were told that in return for this branch the local *geta*-maker had agreed to give him a new pair. For all his fears, his house survived intact and it looked quite unchanged eleven years after I had left it. Today the site is occupied by a small school building.

It was not always easy for foreigners in the provincial towns to get servants, since their ways of living were known to be odd and unaccountable and servants found the hard floors in foreign-style houses painful for their *tabi*-clothed feet – *tabi* being Japanese-style socks. That particular objection, however, did not apply to our house and, again through the kindness of our colleague acting as an intermediary, we engaged a middle-aged widow as housekeeper. She knew little or nothing about foreign ways, except what she had learned from her daughter who had spent some time as a children's nurse with a French family. Nonetheless, she was intelligent and she showed herself ready and quick in learning new things. She seemed to have no prejudices against foreigners, whom she found on the whole interesting and amusing. She had a keen sense of humour and this tided us over innumerable misunderstandings. Like all Japanese servants, she was entirely trustworthy and loyal.

She had been well brought up and knew all the etiquette of seemly behaviour. We relied on her for advice in most of our transactions with people in the neighbourhood. Representatives of the village called on us periodically for subscriptions. There was, for instance, a common interest in

A Bachelor's Household in Nagoya

safeguarding our village against fire and money was needed to pay for the annual visit of the fire brigade to the national shrine at Ise, where they could pray for divine protection. After the Great Earthquake of 1923, the village had to play its part in raising money for relief. Our housekeeper always knew precisely how much we were expected to give and we gave it. She also saw that we were never overcharged when we made a purchase. Whenever we had a caller, she would be sure to produce the appropriate refreshment, even if she had to borrow the ingredients and utensils from neighbours. She knew nothing of foreign-style cooking when she arrived so we bought her a cookery book intended for Japanese cooks in foreign households. At the top of each page was the name of a foreign dish; below there was a description in Japanese of how it should be made.

The same method of communication was used by packers of Indian tea for consumption in Japan. Liptons inserted in their canisters a note in Japanese which informed the cook that the colour of the end-product should be identical with that of the wrapper. This was a necessary precaution since Japanese tea is pale in colour and delicate in flavour. For some kinds of tea, boiling water destroys the subtle flavour. Indeed, a special vessel is sometimes employed to cool the boiling water. Liptons were well intentioned but experience taught me that the right colour is a necessary but not a sufficient condition for excellence in tea-making.

Some of the results of our housekeeper's efforts to follow the instructions in the cookery book would have surprised its author. Once we were presented with a rice pudding which differed only from the familiar English dish in that it was strongly flavoured with vinegar. No doubt we deserved what we got for ordering such a misuse of Japan's staple foodstuff. The chief product of the oven consisted of rock cakes which deserved their designation for other reasons than that the first part of our housekeeper's surname was *Iwa* (rock). These eponymous cakes always appeared when we had callers.

Appointment in Japan

As some kinds of Western foodstuffs of good quality were not available locally, we used to buy the more exotic foods – butter, cheese, cooking fat, bacon and Indian tea (red tea as the Japanese call it) – from foreign grocers at Kobe and Yokohama. Our housekeeper thought that our taste for butter was unaccountable and she believed, probably rightly, that foreigners consumed too much fat. Cheese was to her a disgusting food and she used to bring it to table at arm's length calling out "*Kusai, Kusai*" (smelly, smelly). Out of deference to her we soon gave it up. The rest of our supplies came from the variety of little shops in the village. Eggs, chickens (which could be bought in small pieces) and fish were plentiful, and there was a good supply of fruit, including apples, persimmons, grapes, oranges, mandarins, strawberries and *nashi*. The latter had the shape of a large apple and the texture of a pear. Its taste was accurately described by its name which implies a negative, but it was very refreshing in hot weather. The grapes and strawberries, though abundant in season, were not of high quality, and in this respect, as in so many others, Japan has made great progress in the last sixty years. Today Japanese grapes are excellent and so are the strawberries, which are available for ten months of the year.

We seldom bought butcher's meat. Mutton we gave up entirely after one or two luckless experiences. We discovered that the same character was used for designating sheep and goats, and it became evident that our supplier was unaware of any difference. The existence of a single category for sheep and goats must have created what are now called "problems of communication" for the missionaries.

One of our chief suppliers we called the Big Shop, as it was marginally larger than the others. It was a valuable source of village gossip and our housekeeper never came back from a shopping expedition without some titbits – amusing, scandalous, malicious or bawdy. We heard through her what the villagers thought of our colleagues who lived in the neighbourhood, and especially their

A Bachelor's Household in Nagoya

opinion of foreign residents. It is probably as well that tact prevented her from passing on their views of us.

When the shopkeepers called to deliver provisions they seemed to enjoy lingering in our kitchen, where they were much entertained by our mistakes in speaking their language. They were particularly amused when we dropped into the Nagoya dialect. In 1936, on my first return visit to Japan, my wife and I went to look at my former home. As we passed by the Big Shop, the proprietor recognised me and was at once all smiles and kind greetings. Neither he nor his shop seemed to have changed during the interval. He was surrounded by his children and when he asked, as politeness demanded, how many I had, I gave him a number which put me ahead.

Although we had engaged only one servant, in practice we often found others ministering to our wants. From time to time Mrs Iwata brought her daughter or one of her sisters to stay with her, and they then became part of the household. A married sister who occasionally paid a visit was a most vigorous personality with the assured manners of a woman of the world, quite unlike the typical demure and retiring wife. We found that she had been a *geisha* who had made a good marriage with a prosperous timber merchant.

Our housekeeper entertained the strangest ideas of the West. She never really grasped the differences between the various Europeans who lived in Nagoya and only gradually became aware that some Japanese ways of living and Japanese ideas about life seemed odd to Westerners. Her artlessness made her a most valuable source of objective information about Japanese customs and attitudes. She enjoyed gossip and, like most Japanese, was a realist in her social judgements. She told us all about the difficulties of a local family where the mother was more than usually jealous of her daughter-in-law. She pointed out with relish the *besso* (villa) where a rich businessman had installed a *geisha*. She was patriotic and had no doubt about Japan's superiority to other nations.

Appointment in Japan

This superiority, she thought, extended even to religion. Once when her daughter was ill, she came to us for advice and we recommended a visit to the hospital. She distrusted hospitals, however, and when she heard that a local shrine was dedicated to a god who was able to cure the disease in question, she took the daughter along with her for prayer and offerings. A few days later she announced that the god's intervention had been effective and that the daughter was cured. We expressed some incredulity, but she explained patiently that the Japanese pantheon with its thousands of gods, each with special attributes or functions, was necessarily superior to Christianity where one god has to do everything. I knew about the advantages of specialisation in economic affairs, but I had never before thought that the principle might be held to have an application in the sphere of theology.

Mrs Iwata had an inexhaustible store of anecdote and legend. She occasionally played on the *koto* (a stringed instrument that rested on the floor) and I found that she knew most of the folk songs that Lafcadio Hearn and other writers on Japan had collected a generation or two earlier. She also told us about the village life in her youth – in the eighteen-seventies and eighties. She remembered that, in those days, the wives and daughters of farmers from the plains nearby gathered cotton which was ginned, spun and woven at home. By the 1920s, of course, Japan had long been importing all the cotton she needed, and the spinning of cotton yarn and the weaving of standard-width cotton had gone into the mills. But there were still many cottages in our neighbourhood where women were producing narrow cotton cloth for *yukata* on hand looms.

It did not take us long to learn the technique of living in a Japanese house. The bathroom, in the old style, contained a stone slab and a small circular wooden tub into which the metal side of a stove protruded. The bath was filled with water from the kitchen pump, a fire of lignite was lit in the stove and was fed from the kitchen until the temperature of the water was judged to be sufficiently high (which was

A Bachelor's Household in Nagoya

excessively hot). When the signal was given, the most honourable member of the household entered the bathroom, scooped water from the bath with a small wooden pail and, standing on the stone slab, carried out his ablutions. After rinsing off all the soap, he finally got into the bath, crouched down and parboiled himself, taking care not to approach too near the exposed metal of the stove. As the dimensions of the bath had not been devised with bulky Europeans in mind, it was easy to get scorched.

This process was followed by other members of the household in descending order of status. Our housekeeper, who, like all Japanese, had a strong sense of hierarchy, insisted that the right order should be followed. Whatever the circumstance, she rejected with horror any suggestion that she should go first. However, she was not above using the convention as a pretext for the avoidance of social inconveniences. Thus, if she felt that an afternoon caller had taken up enough of our time, she came to announce that the bath was ready. The caller then had to take the hint and go.

Quite often she and other members of her family who happened to be staying, preferred to go to the local bath house, where all sat together in a large communal bath tub and shared the jokes and gossip of the neighbourhood. In my case this experience was limited to the occasions when I stayed in Japanese inns in the mountains or in country towns. In those days, in country bath houses and the bath rooms of country inns, bathing was mixed. In the more highly sophisticated towns men and women usually entered by different doors, but, I was told, often met in a common bath tub, although this was sometimes divided by a rope stretched diagonally across it. The daily bath, taken in the evening, had long been an important event in the life of Japanese of all classes – important as a social occasion as well as for its ritualistic and hygienic properties. After the Great Earthquake of 1923 the population of Tokyo attached priority to the restoration of the bath houses. Perhaps it was as well that there was little intercourse between Japan and the West during the many centuries in which even the European aristocracy remained unwashed! The elegant nobles and merchant princes of the *Genroku* period (1688–1704) could hardly have borne being in the same room as the courtiers of Louis XIV.

What is and what is not tolerable in matters of hygiene is, however, largely a matter of habit or convention, and Japanese standards were not equally high in every aspect of their living. We used to get ice from the village to cool our drinks in the summer. One day I happened to be passing the shop which sold it and I found that the proprietor was lifting a block of ice from a pit almost on his doorstep and adjacent to the drain. Conditions in our kitchen would probably not have been thought satisfactory by a British housewife. A bad habit of more general importance was that of hawking and spitting in public.

From time to time odd creatures emerged from the *tatami*. To the dismay of our housekeeper, they occasionally included *geji-geji* – large centipedes which were said to be poisonous. We were much troubled by mosquitoes on summer evenings and were only half successful in our attempts to protect ourselves by burning spiral-shaped incense sticks. Of course, we had to sleep under mosquito nets from June to October. Now and then, rats pursued by a weasel scampered across the ceilings, like a stampede of cattle. Occasionally one of them was detected observing us through a knot hole. Once a rat spent the night in the coat pocket of my friend and leapt out when he felt for his watch in the morning. When they invaded our rooms at night, we set traps and so reduced their numbers. During the annual *o-soji* (house-cleaning) a few of their corpses were always uncovered.

The *o-soji* was a sensible institution. In the interests of hygiene, every householder was under a legal obligation to clean his house thoroughly once a year, and the police ensured that he did so. The house had, in effect, to be taken to pieces. The *tatami*, floorboards, *shoji*, *fusuma*, *amado* and all the other components had to be removed. The earth

A Bachelor's Household in Nagoya

beneath the floor and the timbers supporting the roof were exposed and a mere shell or framework of the house was left. All the debris of the past year was removed. Dead vermin were recovered from beneath the house and everything was shaken, swept and dusted. We employed two local farmers to do the job for us, including the dismantling and reassembly of the house. On the completion of an *o-soji* the police came round to inspect. If they were satisfied, they stuck a white label on the doorpost; if not, it meant a red label and the work had to be done again. In our case the inspection was quite perfunctory; it was assumed, perhaps rashly, that the house of a *sensei* would be kept reasonably clean.

Many methods of carrying out common tasks were ingenious in their very simplicity, for the Japanese seemed to be able to dispense with elaborate apparatus. For instance, when *kimono* were laundered they were unpicked, and the constituent pieces, after washing, pasted with rice starch on one of the *amado* which had been removed for the purpose. This was placed in the sun and the cloth was peeled off when dry. It was an effective alternative to ironing. Our housekeeper made frequent use of an instrument which resembled an African potentate's fly whisk. With a succession of rapid strokes she removed the dust from the wooden frames of the *shoji* and ensured that it was fairly distributed over the room.

At the beginning of every winter she set about repairing the rents in the *shoji*. Once she had a lot to do because our puppy had amused himself by jumping through it. On another occasion I myself was the cause of the damage. I slipped down our steep stairs from the *nikai* and collided with the *shoji* at the bottom. These were carried into the garden where they became impaled on a branch of one of our pine trees. The repairs were carried out with patches of translucent paper stuck with rice paste over the damaged squares. At points where extra strength was necessary, Mrs Iwata used double paper and inserted a red maple leaf between them, with charming effect. This practice was not regarded as being in the best of taste.

Besides these practical measures of repair and renovation

which were undertaken at appropriate seasons of the year, there were various ritual performances. Once a year Mrs Iwata would close all the *amado*. Then she would fling them all open quickly and at the same time throw down handfuls of dried beans, calling out as she did so: "*Fuku-wa uchi, oni wa soto*" (fortune in, devils out). By ceremonies such as this, together with her offerings to the kitchen god, she maintained the well-being of the household.

A Japanese house, being without foundations, depends for its stability on the heavy tiled roof which holds it in position during storms. Unfortunately, during serious earthquakes, these roofs can also increase the danger of collapse. Our house swayed and creaked ominously under the impact of strong winds, or whenever there was an earth tremor; yet it did not suffer serious damage, for its timber frame was very flexible. The flexibility of these old-fashioned structures was demonstrated by what happened to the house of an English friend of mine. After a typhoon the house was left leaning at an angle of about 25 degrees from the vertical. The landlord restored the status quo by fixing a steel cable to the apex and pulling the house upright with a winch. The steel cable was then pegged to the ground like a guy rope of a tent. My friend, an engineer, speculated upon the breaking point of the cable and his conclusion, especially during storms, sometimes disquieted the guests whom he used to entertain to lively parties in the *nikai*. The servants, crouching below on the ground floor, were even more alarmed.

It was impossible to lock up a Japanese house. At night, or when we were away, the *amado* were closed and latched, but any determined thief could have forced an entry in a couple of minutes. However, there was no risk of pilferage and the only danger was that presented by the small band of professional thieves. These were desperate characters who did not hesitate to use the knife if challenged by householders. Some Japanese used to place a purse of money under the *tatami* in the *genkan* in the hope that if their home received attention the thief would be content with his

A Bachelor's Household in Nagoya

find. We were warned against trying to tackle an intruder. Several Europeans had been killed or badly hurt through disregarding this advice. However, our household was never troubled by thieves and we had implicit confidence in the honesty of all around us.

A recurrent feature in our lives was the visit from the local policeman. In general, the police were regarded with fear and dislike. Some were over-bearing, and the best of them were inclined to be officious. They considered it their duty to keep a paternal eye on everyone in their parish and paid periodical visits to their charges. Our local policeman was a decent fellow. His duty required him to call on us, but he was obviously somewhat embarrassed on these occasions, for he had heard that foreigners usually resented such attentions. So he always began by explaining that his call was directed to seeing whether we needed any help. His main purpose, however, was obviously to take our measure and to make sure that we were behaving ourselves. We gave him tea and rock cakes, and he then had to try to prolong the interview. On every occasion he asked us the same set of questions – our age, education, family history for several generations back and so on. It was foolish to show impatience under this questioning. Like much else in Japan, it was a convention which one had to accept as part of existence.

In our second year we were the cause of even more serious embarrassment to our poor policeman. This was caused by our straying dog who had been away from the house for some days without his collar, and had probably got into a neglected condition. It happened that just then an *eta* (outcast) was rounding up stray dogs, in company with the policeman, and ours was one of those killed by his club. When the policeman learned to whom the dog belonged, he was very upset since it was he who had given permission. He sent his apologies, but avoided us for some time afterwards.

I had another interesting encounter with a member of his profession. When travelling by train to Ise, the site of one of

Appointment in Japan

the great national shrines, I got into conversation with a policeman who was also on his way there. He accompanied me to the shrine and holy places, showed me how to perform the lustrations and finally delivered me to a pleasant inn on the sea-shore of Futami-ga-ura. He was helpful and genial, but I gained the impression that there was an ulterior motive. Foreigners were known to have strange habits and it was as well to keep an eye on them in their excursions to holy places.

Entertaining Japanese friends at home brought some surprises. We might invite a particular person, but when he arrived, he was likely to be accompanied by several friends or members of his family. One occasion is especially clear in my memory. We had invited a student to lunch with us on a public holiday. At about 10.30 A.M. he put in an appearance accompanied by his prospective father-in-law. A few moments later we greeted his future brother-in-law, and twenty minutes later his fiancée, her mother and a friend of the family arrived. Admittedly they had brought food to supplement our exiguous supplies, but we had not bargained for such an invasion. However, for the rest of the day we simply handed over responsibility for hospitality to the women-folk.

I look back on holiday excursions into the nearby countryside as a kind of procession, with me in the lead accompanied by the friend whom I had invited and behind us a trail of his friends and relations. Time was of little account on these social occasions and punctuality little esteemed. Sometimes when an hour was named for the start of the excursion, I used to ask: "Japanese time, or English time?" No one seemed to be in a hurry.

Much of this has changed, or so it appears to me. Nowadays Japanese are at great pains to be punctual for appointments. Nonetheless, I fancy that there is still a disposition among ordinary people to regard invitations as applicable to groups rather than to individuals.

Peddlers were a notable feature of life in those days and we had calls from a constant succession of them. Some sold

A Bachelor's Household in Nagoya

household goods and foods, such as noodles and bean paste; others, like the blind masseurs, offered services; and yet others, including the occasional Chinese, carried various curios. Most of them announced their presence in the neighbourhood by sounding the pipes, horns, trumpets and whistles traditionally associated with their trade. I particularly liked the pipe-cleaner. As he wheeled his little steam engine, the ears of bystanders were pierced by the shrill whistle made by the escaping steam. This noise ceased when a customer brought him a pipe which he fitted on the valve so that the steam could be forced through it. Some of these itinerant vendors still flourish, but their numbers have much diminished. Many customers buy their noodles from self-service stores. Since the Japanese have given up their tiny tobacco pipes in which they smoked finely-shredded tobacco, the pipe-cleaner's trade has become obsolete. In 1954, however, I came across one of them in Kyoto.

All these activities meant that, although we were not troubled by mechanical noises, ours was by no means a silent neighbourhood. The calls and sounds of the itinerant vendors were supplemented from time to time by the harsh voices of schoolboys reciting their lessons and by the barking of dogs which Japanese seem to tolerate without protest. In summer evenings we could enjoy the more agreeable sounds of musical instruments played by our neighbours – the simple tunes of the *koto*, the more lively rhythms of the *shamisen* coming from the *besso* where the *geisha* was entertaining her patron, and the melancholy notes of the flute from a student's lodging. We missed the song of birds in spring, but we had a surfeit in season of the croaking of frogs, which the Japanese said sounded like the speech of foreigners, and the whirring of the cicadas which closely resembled the noise made by a rather defective two-stroke motor-cycle engine when starting up from cold.

When I last visited the district, in the spring of 1979, I found that what had been a village with a life of its own, had been engulfed by the growth of the city. The farm-land had been built over and new roads had been made. The former site of my house was impossible to identify. There was one survival – the village shrine. The Japanese friends, who were helping me in my pursuit of *temps perdu*, took me up to it. We flung coins into the offertory box, clapped our hands to attract the attention of the god, and bowed our heads. It was a satisfying ritual.

The view from the house was characteristic of that seen by multitudes of Japanese villagers in those days. The buildings were all low and unobtrusive, scattered in groups with the village shrine set amid pine trees in the centre. Beyond them stretched rice fields and upland fields with groves of bamboo dotted here and there. In the evening I used to look westwards from the *nikai* over the flat land and admire the attempts of nature to copy a Hiroshige sky, narrow bands of yellow, red and mauve on the horizon and above the clear cobalt blue.

In the 1920s I could afford the delights of life that Japan offered because, by Japanese standards, I was receiving a high salary and the cost of living for me was low. During term time my total expenditure amounted to between £16 and £18 a month; of course, it would have been greater if I had not shared the household expenses with my colleague. The housekeeper's monthly wages were equivalent to the amount of our rent (£3.50 at the rate of exchange that prevailed in 1922-3). Out of this she found her own rice. When others came to help her we gave them presents. During vacations I travelled extensively and spent more lavishly. While Japanese inns were then very cheap, foreign-style hotels were quite expensive by the standards of the time – about £1 a day *en pension* for most of them. I seldom paid so much, because teachers in government institutions, like civil servants, were given rebates of 10 per cent and upwards on railway fares and hotel bills. All services were very cheap, although the best restaurants of the old style were quite expensive.

During my first year in Japan the yen was over-valued (that is to say, its external value was greater than that

A Bachelor's Household in Nagoya

justified by the internal price-level in relation to that of other countries). Soon after the Earthquake of 1 September 1923, the exchange value of the yen fell in terms of sterling by about 20 per cent. This raised the price of imported goods, including imported food, but did not substantially affect my cost of living. I left Japan in the spring of 1925 and did not return for eleven years. Then I found that, largely in consequence of the World Depression, internal prices had fallen. The exchange value of the yen had also depreciated; it was worth 6p in 1936 compared with 10p in 1922. The prices in yen of food, manufactured goods, services and accommodation were all much lower than in the 1920s, and this fact, together with the undervaluation of the yen in terms of dollars and sterling, meant that the cost of living for foreign residents and visitors had steeply declined. I shall say more about prices and economic conditions in a later chapter.

It was, of course, the foreigners in Japan in that period who had the best of it. The advantages of these low prices were not so obvious to the mass of the people whose incomes also were very low. Many girls in the cotton-spinning mills in the 1930s earned less than one yen a day in addition to their board and lodging and their bi-annual bonuses. Four yen a day (24p) was reckoned a good wage for a highly skilled male worker in large firms. Wages and salaries were on the whole lower in the 1930s than in the 1920s during my first years in Japan and, even then, I had sometimes been taken aback when I heard the salaries of men senior to myself and far better qualified.

III

Town and Country in the 1920s

The city of Nagoya lies about half-way between Osaka and Tokyo on an alluvial plain which runs down to the sea in the South and in the North rises to meet the hills which form part of the core of Central Japan. In the 1920s it had about 750,000 inhabitants. It was the administrative centre of the Aichi Prefecture and, like the adjacent town of Atsuta, it was already a leading port. The climate was pleasant enough in the spring and autumn, and even in winter the days were usually sunny, although after sunset the temperature dropped steeply. The summer, however, was very uncomfortable, hot and moist, especially in June. This is the rainy season, when energy is sapped by the heat and humidity, household goods and shoes acquire a layer of mould, and butter and other foods become rancid. A Japanese friend told me how bewildered he had been in his boyhood when he read an English book which started with a description of children as they ran out to play: "Hurrah for summer!" they cried. Why should they rejoice, he pondered, at the arrival of so disagreeable a season? After he had spent a year in England he was no longer mystified.

Nagoya was one of the chief industrial cities of Japan but it had few features in common with the industrial towns of the Western world. Although its range of manufacturing activities was wide, large factories were few. There were some cotton mills and pottery factories, including the famous Nippon Toki (Noritake) which produced foreign-

Town and Country in the 1920s

style table-ware, mainly for export, and was a pioneer in the introduction of flow production methods and modern kilns in this industry. Among the several substantial engineering works, Mitsubishi's aircraft factory was the most interesting. Here a group of English aeronautical engineers, test pilots and mechanics, most of whom had formerly been employed by Sopwiths, were teaching the Japanese to make aeroplanes. In the neighbourhood there was also a large brewery, for which the Germans provided the technical expertise and, a few miles to the north, a hydro-electric power station to which a few American engineers were attached.

By far the greater part of the industrial output, however, came from small workshops. Domestic industry flourished both in the town and in the surrounding countryside. I had already become interested in economic history. I saw that Nagoya appeared to be at the stage of industrial development through which Britain had passed in the first half of the nineteenth century. There was the added attraction that many of the products of these small workshops were of a kind unfamiliar to Western markets – *shoji*, *tatami*, screens, low tables and cabinets, pottery of unusual design, paper fans, *geta* and shrines for the household gods. Some of the exotic products were of fairly recent origin. For instance, Nagoya had become a well-known centre of *cloisonné* manufacture, a product which had been introduced by a German about fifty years earlier. All these activities were revealed simply by a stroll in any direction, for much of the work went on in the front rooms of the dwelling houses or in small sheds attached to them. As these were open to the street, no detail was hidden from the curious.

Much of the work was done by hand and the craftsmen used what were to me quite unfamiliar tools. As electricity was available everywhere, the employment of little electric motors to drive simple machines was already widespread. There were numerous small metal and engineering workshops equipped with two or three drilling machines or lathes. In all of them the work seemed to go on far into the

Appointment in Japan

night. However late I returned to my house, the local *geta*-maker's workshop seemed to be in operation, and however early I set out in the morning, the potter was arranging his bowls to dry in the morning sun.

I observed, however, that the work was not continuous. The craftsman spent much of his time in sitting over his *hibachi*, smoking his little pipe and sipping tea with his clients or cronies.

As in all economies at that stage of development, the children of the household had their tasks. Every day on my way to the College, I passed a cottage where small children were helping their parents to paste labels on to match boxes. Since many of the workers in the small shops squatted on mats to do their work, certain processes and methods were adapted to this posture. I admired the skill of the girls in a clothing workshop who used their toes for holding the cloth while they sewed with their fingers.

Particular trades tended to be concentrated in particular quarters of the town, and there were a few places near Nagoya which specialised in a single product. For example, the ancient town of Seto, to which the art of pottery making had been brought from China a thousand years ago, was composed almost entirely of small pottery workshops which manufactured mainly cheap Japanese-style table ware (*Seto-mono* is the Japanese word for pottery). Ichinomya, which was not far from Nagoya, was becoming a centre for the manufacture of light worsted cloth in small mills. The countryside which I explored on foot seemed crowded with industrial activities. Small weaving sheds, reeling mills, potteries and metal workshops were to be encountered in unexpected places. Occasionally, in what seemed remote spots, I came across a large factory with dormitories to house the workers. The old and the new, the putting-out system, according to which a merchant-employer organised the work of dependent domestic craftsmen, and the factory system, flourished side by side.

The physical conditions of production were reflected in the appearance of the city as a whole. There were a few wide streets, which were usually tram routes, but the majority were narrow and without pavements. In the winter they became muddy and the advantage of the high wooden *geta*, out of which one could step on going indoors, was obvious. The majority of the buildings, including all the dwelling houses, were single or double-storied wooden structures. The few tall buildings stood out in contrast. Of these, the oldest were made of brick, but concrete was used for all later construction. The town was dominated by the Keep of Nagoya Castle, surrounded by a moat and massive stone walls. It was a splendid sight, lofty, white and graceful, and it was surmounted by two golden dolphins. Like almost everything else in Nagoya, the Castle was destroyed during the Second World War. It has since been rebuilt in concrete, and it still looks splendid at a distance, although it no longer towers over the new city as it did over the old. The dolphins have inspired a dance with which the Nagoya *geisha* entertain their patrons. Two *geisha* conclude this dance by standing on their heads and assuming, with their heels in the air, the posture of the dolphins on the roof of the castle.

The Nagoya of the 1920s, taken as a whole, could not be regarded as a beautiful city despite its name which means "famous, ancient place". Like most large towns in Japan, its aesthetic charm resided in detail rather than in broad vistas. Beauty and squalor rubbed shoulders, and it may be that the contrasts, which were everywhere forced on the observer's attention, enhanced his pleasure. In walks along dull and featureless streets I was constantly delighted by the unexpected sight of the exquisite porch of a house or restaurant with a foreground arrangement of a pine tree and rocks and a tiny stream, or a stone basin into which water was trickling through a bamboo pipe. These beauties still exist, but they have to be sought for. Then, they were met with at every turn.

What was novel to me was, of course, commonplace to the ordinary Japanese. He has always shown curiosity about new things and he was sometimes unable to discriminate between the quality of the innovations that struck his attention. It is ironical that, while I went about admiring gems of traditional domestic architecture, Japanese flocked to see the few foreign-style houses in our neighbourhood. One of them, the home of an American missionary, though ill-proportioned and badly built, always attracted, on holidays, large numbers of amateur photographers and other sightseers.

Most Europeans who came to Japan in the 1920s travelled via the ports. As their ship usually spent some days at Hong Kong and Shanghai, they could scarcely avoid making comparisons between the Japanese and the Chinese scene. I recorded my impressions soon after my arrival in Nagoya. I had been enthralled by the lively and picturesque disorder of Chinese streets, even though I had been repelled by the evidence of extreme poverty and squalor that they presented. Japanese towns, in day-time at any rate, lacked the colour of the Chinese, but they looked cleaner and it was obvious at once that their inhabitants lived on a higher plane of material well-being than other Asians. Japanese dress, except that of children and young girls, was more sombre than I had expected, but the people in the streets were generally well-groomed. I especially noted the striking contrast between the Chinese and the Japanese rickshaw coolies, the former grubby and unkempt, the latter clean and neat in their dark, tight-fitting costumes.

I have already recorded my excitement at my first glimpse of a Japanese city at night. The frail and sometimes ramshackle structures were concealed in the shadows, and the bright lights disclosed the interiors of shops and restaurants. In the main street of Nagoya they shone on an avenue of willow trees. Under them were the booths and stalls where all kinds of household goods, cooked foods and curios could be purchased. I never tired of strolling in the evening among the friendly orderly crowds, listening to the transactions at the stalls and observing craftsmen at their trades. The noise was intensified and the colours enhanced

Town and Country in the 1920s

as one approached the neighbourhood of the cinemas and theatres, adorned with large paper lanterns. A few steps further would carry one into a different world, the peace of a temple courtyard where the only sounds were the murmurs of prayer, the clapping of hands to invite the attention of the god, and the sonorous boom as a devotee, or curious sightseer, swung a wooden beam at the great bell.

Some discoveries were surprising rather than aesthetically attractive. Once when I was wandering about Osaka I found myself in a relic of Victorian England. The quarter into which I had strayed consisted of several streets of redbrick villas with bay windows and small, railed-off front gardens. There was a church in Victorian Gothic and a building that might have served as a parish hall. I had stumbled on the Concession where foreign merchants lived in the early modern period. These merchants, for many years, handled a high proportion of Japan's international trade. Here they reproduced, as far as they could, the environment which they had left behind in Europe. As I looked closer at this survival from a long-dead era, I saw that the premises were now used as offices and warehouses by Japanese firms. The families of the Smiths and MacDonalds had been replaced by the clerks of Suzuki or Saito.

I suppose that these houses were demolished many years ago. Today the best witnesses of that period are to be found in the *Meiji* Village, not far from Nagoya. To this place there has been transferred a selection of buildings typical of the early *Meiji* period, including a brick church, a wooden house in colonial style once occupied by a famous political leader, a military hospital, a bank and also several houses of traditional design. The tour of the Village can be made in a tramcar of the *Meiji* vintage. I left the place with the rueful conviction that Japan owed little of aesthetic value to her early contact with the Western world.

As Nagoya was a conservative city, it was not entirely representative of Japan in the early 1920s. Yet even Tokyo, which was more modern in its layout and where the administrative and business quarters resembled those of

Appointment in Japan

European towns, was in the main a city of low wooden houses, very similar to those in Nagoya. Few of the roads, even in the central part of the capital, were macadamised and the side roads were unmade. Since there was very little heavy traffic at that time, this was no particular hardship.

The place that attracted me most from the time of my first visit was Kyoto. Although some of its charm and all its peace have now departed, the glories of its palaces, temples, shrines and gardens remain untarnished to this day. In the 1920s it was not only its more obvious beauties that fascinated me, for I was never tired of looking at the people as they went about their ordinary occupations. The Nishijin quarter of the town was the traditional centre for the manufacture of the first silks for *obi* and *kimono*. The work was done in small workshops on hand-looms where the most intricate and beautiful patterns of cloth were produced. The weaver worked with numerous shuttles containing yarn of different colours. Having threaded these through the warp, he drew the weft together with combs, or with his finger-nails, which were cut in grooves for the purpose. The merchants who placed orders with the weavers bought their designs from talented artists who frequented Kyoto. For the higher quality goods only one item of each design was produced. The products and designs were on display at the Nishijin Museum or showroom, which was run by a local guild. I once had the privilege of attending a meeting of the council of this guild when it was discussing policy.

The dyers and finishers were also highly-skilled craftsmen. Their small workshops backed on to the river, and it is said that the state of the Kyoto silk trade could be judged by the extent to which the waters were stained with dyes. Kyoto was the seat of a great wholesaler, Marubeni, who always had on display in his show-rooms a most gorgeous collection of silks. Since then the silk trade has decayed, or at least has fallen steeply in industrial importance. The shortage of craftsmen has enforced changes in methods, and weaving processes have been mechanised. In the

Town and Country in the 1920s

Nishijin quarter, Japanese have been replaced to a considerable extent by Koreans, who can still be recruited at relatively low wages. The great silk wholesale house has become, under the name of Marubeni-Iida, one of the largest general merchant firms in Japan and is engaged in exporting the whole range of Japan's industrial products and in importing raw materials. Its development typifies the adaptability of Japan to the new world.

The silk trade was only one example of the many craft industries that flourished in Kyoto. Small potteries produced hand-thrown ware in a bewildering variety of design and the products were fired in co-operatively-run kilns. Some of the goods were expensive, but many of them were of a kind in everyday use in Japanese households. They were all tasteful and some exquisitely beautiful.

In 1922 Japanese women wore their national dress almost universally and the elaborate formal coiffure, which varied with age and marital status, was still common. They had given up blackening their teeth on marriage, a practice designed, presumably, to make them unattractive to possible lovers, but among older women this disfigurement could still be seen. The men also commonly wore Japanese dress at home, although in banks and offices they generally preferred European-style suits. The labourers were dressed in cotton tunics (*happi*) marked in characters with the name and style of their employer, along with tight cotton trousers. In summer they, and the peasants who brought produce into the town, wore little other than loin cloths and sweat towels. Students in all grades of school and college were usually to be seen in dark-blue uniforms and the schoolgirls also wore Western-style dresses with heavy, dark-blue pleated skirts and sailor collars. The police, railway officials and, of course, the soldiers, all had foreign-style uniforms.

The Great Earthquake of 1923 was something of a dividing line sartorially. After that disaster, foreign dress spread rapidly among men, at any rate in the middle class. The women, though, continued to prefer Japanese dress, except when, as factory operatives or, in the 1930s, as bus conductors, their employers provided them with uniforms. Nagoya, being a provincial town and rather conservative in outlook, was less advanced in dress than Tokyo. Yet even in the capital, it was not until after the Second World War that foreign dress became the usual wear for both sexes. Japanese dress continues to be worn on ceremonial occasions – at the Kabuki theatre, for example, and by women at weddings. Outside the home, it is now the exception.

In the 1920s a mother always carried her baby tied in a shawl on her back. This sensible practice left her arms free and had other advantages. The baby reinforced her effectiveness as a battering ram when she was trying to force her way through crowds, and on tramcars it cleared the way to a seat. In all struggles of this sort the baby slept on unperturbed. Snug in its shawl, it hardly knew that it was born. With the adoption of Western dress, mothers have been obliged to convey their offspring in perambulators.

Some foreigners used to be amused at the widespread practice of wearing gauze pads or masks to cover the nose and mouth during the winter months as a safeguard against colds and influenza. Even the soldiers were so equipped. It seemed, to a layman, a sensible precaution against the spread of infection, but I never discovered whether the medical profession approved of it. Recently the practice has been revived as a protection against a new hazard, namely the smog in Tokyo and other cities.

When I first arrived nearly everyone used a *karakasa*, the paper umbrella which could be adjusted to give different degrees of protection against the driving rain. *Karakasa* were convenient, efficient and beautifully made, with articulated bamboo ribs and oiled paper usually printed with a traditional design. These have become difficult to come by. Since they are hand-made, they are expensive, and users now prefer factory-made steel and nylon umbrellas. A few years ago, when I was walking along the main street of Kyoto on a rainy day, I noticed that I was almost the only person carrying a *karakasa*.

Town and Country in the 1920s

In my early days in Japan one could buy for a penny or so large sheets of thick oiled paper with tapes attached. These served as most admirable waterproof capes for walkers. They could be adjusted to cover one's rucksack and yet they allowed plenty of ventilation. When not in use they could be folded up into small compass. Many of these traditional Japanese devices fulfil Alfred Duggan's excellent definition of efficiency: "The exact adjustment of means to ends, with nothing wasted."

The changes that have occurred since those days have made the Japanese scene less picturesque and Europeans who knew Japan at that time deplore them. However, many powerful influences have combined to bring them about. The *kimono* was admirably suited to the Japanese way of living, but foreign dress was more convenient for many workaday purposes. Moreover, the trend towards Western furnishings (for example, the greater use of chairs and tables) has reduced the appeal of Japanese dress.

Before the Second World War, the Western clothes then available did not look well on Japanese women, but after the War there were marked improvements in quality and style. When I first went to Nagoya, most Japanese did not know how to wear Western garments and they were often put to unconventional uses. Once I sat opposite a Japanese in a tramcar, an elderly man who had just acquired a pair of ladies' combinations with lace edges; he was lifting up his *kimono* and proudly showing them off to his admiring companions. Even the department stores of the 1950s still found it necessary to provide charts and instructions in their women's clothing sections to indicate the order in which foreign garments should be put on.

Undoubtedly the most powerful force in bringing about changes in dress has been price. Although even before the War the highest quality silks were expensive, most kinds of clothing were very cheap. After the Second World War, wages in the textile and clothing trades rose steeply. In the manufacture of standardised foreign-style garments, the economies of large-scale mechanised production have compensated for increased labour costs. Such methods were not applicable in general to the labour-intensive Japanese-style clothing trade, although there were a few exceptions, e.g. the manufacture of *tabi* (Japanese socks).

Relative price changes have played a major part in bringing about modifications in the Japanese way of living. While the traditional house was sparsely furnished, most of the utensils and furnishings in common use were the work of craftsmen. This applied also to the components of the house itself, the *tatami, shoji* and *fusuma*. With the rise in the price of labour in the last twenty-five years all these articles have soared in price, while the development of modern industries has lowered the price of goods to which large-scale, capital-intensive methods of manufacture could be applied.

The various changes are interrelated. Foreign-style furnishings strengthened the tendency to wear foreign clothing. Changes in the diet required changes in the utensils used. Modern methods of heating affected clothing and furnishings. In my day, when it was almost impossible to heat a Japanese house in winter, people dealt with the problem simply by putting on more and more layers of clothing, including quilted *kimono*, as the weather became colder. With modern heating there is no need for this expedient.

The shortage and high cost of domestic service nowadays means that it has become more difficult for the Japanese housewife to prepare elaborate Japanese meals. The commuter eats bread for his breakfast, since this enables him to get off to work more quickly. Those who knew Japan in the past cannot observe these changes without nostalgia. It could not be expected, though, that a way of life which reflected the country's high aesthetic tradition could survive into an age of rapid industrial development. The Japanese preference for unostentatious or even austere beauty, a concept which may be expressed by the word *shibui*, has fallen victim to technological progress. At the same time, when I reflect on the hard and frugal lives which the majority of people led in the early days, I am conscious also of the blessings of that progress.

Even in the 1920s the streets were crowded with traffic, but except in the main thoroughfares which carried the tramlines, there was nothing to prevent pedestrians from sauntering down the middle of roads at will. Waggons drawn by oxen or horses were the chief vehicles used for moving heavy goods, while lighter articles were delivered in carts pulled by men, sometimes with the assistance of dogs. The main instrument of local delivery was the bicycle. I, like all other foreign residents, marvelled at the skill of the errand boys in balancing high and heavy loads on their machines, loads which might consist of a bale of cloth or a tall tower of lunch boxes. I remember one boy who used to deliver goods to us, sweeping around obstacles in his path without checking speed and whistling airs from *Carmen*, a popular opera in Japan at that time.

The Japanese bicycle had to be robust to carry the heavy loads over the ill-made roads. Sometime in the early 1930s, I read with scepticism newspaper reports that Japan was exporting to West Africa bicycles that fell apart after a few months' use. I found on enquiry that there was, in fact, no inconsistency between those reports and my own observation. The bicycles sold in Japan were well-made, sturdy and quite expensive. In the models sold for export, which were priced as low as thirty shillings, solid drawn tubes had been replaced by welded tubes and forgings by brittle iron castings. Japan has never been slow in adapting her production to the diverse demands of her several markets!

In the *Tokugawa* period (1600–1868), Nagoya had been a centre of power and, in spite of its incursions into modern industry, the past survived there more vigorously than in the capital or the ports. Even the language spoken had a number of peculiarities. The cost of living was low compared with that of other great cities and the people had the reputation of being careful with their money – the Japanese Scots, as they have been called. This reputation was borne out by the conduct of my landlord which I have described

Appointment in Japan

earlier. Mr Tanzan Ishibashi (Prime Minister from 1956–57), when editor of the *Oriental Economist*, told me that the frugality of the typical Nagoya citizen made it difficult for an outsider to judge his income by reference to his manner of living. Mr Ishibashi added that the sales of his journal in Nagoya suffered because the practice of reading it free at the bookstalls was so widespread there. Since then I have been told by Japanese friends that Nagoya is a rather self-centred and clannish place. An outsider approaches it with circumspection and does well to equip himself with introductions to established citizens before he attempts to do business there.

I must confess that my own reception in Nagoya concealed these aspects of its character from me. Even the tax office turned a blind eye to my obligations. The generosity with which I have been treated on my subsequent visits suggests that meanness is the last infirmity which I should attribute to the people of Nagoya. Perhaps their prosperity has excited the jealousy of other places.

The quarter in which I lived, and in which the College was situated, was on the extreme edge of the town. The appearance of the countryside adjacent to my village was, of course, entirely strange to me. There were no meadows with grazing herds and no hedges. Nearby there was a region called Gokiso, which was famous for the cultivation of *daikon*, a large radish which, when pickled, gives flavour to every Japanese meal. I arrived in Nagoya just after the *daikon* had been harvested and when they were being dried before pickling. All over the district the great roots were hanging from the pine trees, and for a moment I mistook them for some monstrous unknown fruit.

In addition to the upland fields there were the paddies: patches of mud and water in the spring until the shoots of the young rice appeared, and in the autumn a brown sea of heavy grain. When I walked along the narrow paths bordering the fields I observed the peasants knee-deep in water transplanting the seedlings or, after the harvest, breaking up the heavy soil with their hoes. In the growing season they

Town and Country in the 1920s

could be seen ladling out the night-soil from wooden containers. The stench of this fertiliser detracted considerably from the pleasure of walks in agricultural areas.

In busy times the peasants worked by moonlight. Indeed, their labour seemed almost continuous, punctuated only by the national holidays and local festivals. Their wide straw hats and straw capes (*mino*) protected them from sun and rain and most of them also wore straw footgear (*zori*). Farming was a job of hard manual labour, for the peasants had few draught animals and no power machinery except irrigation pumps and rice-hulling apparatus. The wooden and plaster farmhouses with roofs of deep thatch were a delight to the eye. They and the farm implements – mainly the products of village industry – blended harmoniously with the scene.

The sturdy mountain villages, where the shingled or bark-covered roofs of the houses were held down by large stones, were seemly additions to the loveliness of the natural setting. I became especially fond of visiting them. Although they were characteristically Japanese, there seemed nevertheless to be an affinity between them and the mountain villages of Europe. Perhaps the challenge of the mountains evokes the same defences and responses in all countries. The Japanese love their mountains and admire those who dwell in them. They have a saying: "Heroes come from the mountains."

Outside the more thickly populated areas, the appearance of the countryside has not greatly changed, and a superficial observer might think that rural Japan had preserved its ancient character. In fact, the changes have been profound. Agriculture is now highly mechanised and the ploughing is done by small tractors which operate even in the flooded fields. The implements and furnishings found in the farm buildings are no longer the products of rural craftsmanship. Most of them are factory made, and the farmer's household enjoys the use of all the familiar gadgets of our time. His grown-up sons and daughters go to work in neighbouring factories on motor bicycles and the work of the farm is left to their elders. There is a saying: "*San-chan Nogyo*" – "farming left to three old people, grandfather, grandmother and mother". It has been estimated that sixty per cent of the income of a typical farming family is earned by non-agricultural pursuits.

The peasants, once a breed distinct from the urban workers, and with a standard of living far inferior to theirs, have been swept by industrial progress and the government's policy of protection into a new world where they meet the townsmen on equal terms. In my day they were uneasy during their infrequent encounters with urban ways. They still kept to the old lunar calendar and celebrated the Chinese New Year. At that time and on certain other holidays, parties of countryfolk dressed in freshly laundered *kimono* poured into Nagoya and wandered about gazing in bewilderment at the sights before them. The traffic was a puzzle, and some of them were liable to be upset when, having boarded a tramcar, they found that it would not take them to any place they happened to name. At the time of *O-bon* (the Festival of the Dead) in midsummer, there was feasting in the villages and fires were lit to guide the ancestral spirits to the family shrines.

The agricultural land in the vicinity of the College merged on one side with a wide extent of hilly, untilled land, covered with bamboo, pines and scrub. In the shelter of the woods there were temples, shrines and a few simple restaurants and tea-houses. During my walks over this country I often used to call at one or other of these tea-houses, where I would chat to the proprietor and his family while drinking green tea and eating rice cakes. Like all Japanese on meeting a stranger, they liked to be able to place him in a niche. So whenever I stopped at a place where I was not known, I was plied with questions about my age, family, children, country, occupation, purpose in coming to Japan, and so forth. The questions remind me of the opening words of A. E. Housman's parody of a Greek tragedy:

Town and Country in the 1920s

O suitably-attired-in-leather-boots
Head of a traveller, wherefore, seeking whom,
Whence, by what way, how purposed, art thou come
To this well-nightingaled vicinity?

Substitute the cicada for the nightingale and we are present at an encounter in Japan in the 1920s. Once curiosity had been satisfied and ignorance about my status and function had been dispelled, relations became friendly and easy.

Few days passed without some strange or interesting sight or encounter. Sometimes I was impressed by incongruities. I recall meeting a band of tall and graceful Koreans in white flowing robes who looked as if they were on their way to take part in a religious ceremony. When I later came across them they were packing the ballast round the tramlines! They worked slowly and deliberately together, timing the strokes of their picks to the measure of the shanty-man who led them. Occasionally small groups of old ladies, their hair protected against dust by white head-cloths, were to be seen squatting by the tramlines, removing pebbles and grit from the grooves with metal chop-sticks. Demonstrations to further some cause or other were frequent and certain days were given over to them. Once I found that a procession of highly decorated tramcars was a demonstration to celebrate Birth Control Day. This had been organised by groups troubled by the rapid increase in the country's population.

Usually the pageants were of a traditional character, like the spring festival organised by the men of Mizuho-cho, my village. Early one morning a procession formed up at the village shrine and then set out on a tour of all the houses. It was headed by a villager carrying the symbol of spring, a young bamboo, its leaves decorated with coloured strips of paper. He was followed by two musicians, one playing a flute and the other beating a drum. Behind the musicians came the villagers pulling small carts filled with rice cakes. They sang and shouted, excited with *sake* and the spirit of spring. After they had completed their journey, the cakes were distributed among the children, and the adults took time off for other amusements.

Some festivals were far more elaborate than our local jollifications. The Kobe port festival, for example, gave the onlooker vivid representations of characters and scenes from the past as well as a demonstration of present-day activities. Every period in the port's history and all classes and manners of men and women were commemorated. Even the local *geisha* and prostitutes appeared in costumes fashionable at different times. Among all the traditional scenes, the top hats and frock coats of those who were taking the parts of the American consuls, who settled in Japan soon after the opening of the country, were especially striking.

In the religious festivals young men, inspired by the local deities, rushed to and fro, pulling the gaily decorated vehicles which carried the sacred emblems. They and the onlookers seemed to be on familiar terms with their gods. There was boisterous good humour rather than reverence. On one occasion when I was watching a religious procession winding its way among the Nagoya crowds, a Shinto priest caught my eye. I recognised him as a neighbour whom I occasionally visited. He called the procession to a halt, jumped down from his lofty seat, shook me by the hand and offered me a cigarette. No one except myself seemed to detect any incongruity in this behaviour.

It was quite usual in those days for players of *shakuhachi* (flutes) to wander from village to village. Some of them were priests who begged for alms at the houses before which they played. Often their identity was concealed by basket-like straw hats (*komuso*) which completely covered their faces. This was an ancient practice. In the old times, I was told, spies assumed this garb when they wanted to penetrate into enemy territory. When I first saw these mendicants I thought that their method of concealing their identity was peculiar to Japan but, a few years ago, at Cahirciveen in County Kerry, I watched a procession in celebration of the region's history, with special emphasis on the struggles against the English. Several young participants in the procession wore headgear very similar to that of these Japanese flute players.

The Japanese love of ritual was the source of many of the ceremonies and colourful scenes. At New Year the houses were decorated with pine branches and paper emblems; at the time of the Boys' Festival in May paper models of carp hung from poles outside the houses. A crescendo was reached at the time of the Crown Prince's wedding in 1924. All Japan was *en fête*. Almost every street was adorned with bright banners and at night with paper lanterns, some of enormous size. Crowds flocked to the temples for religious observances. Stages were erected wherever there was space, and jugglers, actors, dancers, musicians and singers gave performances. Parades headed by drums and flutes were held and from time to time there passed through the streets horse-drawn floats in which were sitting *geisha* in superb *kimono*. In Tokyo, the Shimbashi *geisha* gave outdoor performances of dancing and song on stages erected for the purpose. On the hills above some of the towns – Kobe, for example – emblems or designs were picked out at night by electric lamps. In some places, famous scenes from Japanese history or tradition were re-enacted. I remember that a group of schoolboys took the parts of the Forty-Seven *Ronin* (masterless *Samurai*) who are celebrated in the most famous of the Kabuki plays, *Chushingura*. The official ceremonies included the announcement of the nuptials at the three great national Shinto shrines and offerings to the deities

The Japanese, so restrained in their general demeanour, then as now, had the capacity to relax in their leisure moments. They seemed, for a space, to be able to throw their cares and ambitions aside and to become gay and spontaneous. In those distant days when the towns were free of dangerous traffic, the main streets were places of enjoyment and entertainment as well as for leisurely sauntering among the stalls and booths. In Tokyo, the *ginbura*, the evening stroll along the Ginza, was even more fascinating than its counterpart in Nagoya, for the stalls were more varied and numerous and the objects displayed more attractive. The present generation is not allowed (perhaps it does not wish) to enjoy this simple pleasure which its fathers took for granted. The stalls have been banished from the Ginza and from the thoroughfares of other towns. The motor vehicle has claimed another victim.

I soon realised that the threat of recurrent national disasters lay behind the façade of tranquillity. Every year earthquakes, typhoons or fires took a heavy toll of life and property. The flimsy houses were often blown down by storms. Indeed, my very first sight of the harbour districts of Nagoya was of a wide area of devastation, with hundreds of houses flattened by a recent typhoon. Fire was an ever-present menace. Once a house caught fire it was quickly destroyed, for most of the material used in its construction was highly inflammable.

In my first year at Nagoya, several houses in the neighbourhood were burnt to the ground, and I recorded an example of these disasters in detail. One evening, I was aroused by the clanging of the fire bell which, in my village as in most others, hung from a high branch of a pine tree near the shrine, and was reached by a tall ladder. I hurried out to find a neighbour's house ablaze. He and his family had already removed most of their household goods with the help of the crowd that had collected. Soon the flames had devoured the *tatami*, swept up the *shoji* and risen high up above the roof, threatening the adjacent house. This was a fairly large building, and its proprietor was standing in the *nikai* looking out in apprehension on the nearby blaze. Then the crowd divided and on the path leading from the shrine a man came running, carrying on his shoulder a long bamboo stick. It was hung with multi-coloured streamers and had a triangular metal plate, engraved with Chinese characters, fixed to the apex. The stick was attached to that part of the neighbour's house which was nearest to the fire. The crowd cheered, for the danger of the fire spreading was now averted, and attention could be given to the burning house itself. Buckets of water were thrown on the blazing timbers and a hand pump arrived to lend its aid. Soon the house was burned to the ground, but this was not the end of the matter.

The next morning the villagers flocked to the shrine to thank the god for being spared their houses. In the evening they collected together the unburnt fragments of the house and, having lit a bonfire, proceeded to eat and drink in merriment through the night. The ritual was concluded when the unfortunate owner of the house – now a heap of charred ruins – made the round of his neighbours to thank them for their help in coping with the fire. He handed each of us a gift in the form of a packet of stamped postcards, just as he had done a few months earlier on taking up the occupation of the house. His visit was followed by that of a string of acquaintances. They wished me to know of their feelings of anxiety for me as my house was so near the fire. Finally, the owner of a local grocery shop sent me a little bottle of *sake* to restore my equanimity after the strain of the harrowing experience. It was all a touching demonstration of neighbourliness, although I was left with the uneasy feeling that those who had merely been exposed to the risk received more comfort than the family that had lost its property.

I was never able to discover why a calamity had been made an occasion for a party. Maybe it was to bring some comfort to the unfortunate family now homeless, or possibly those whose houses had been in danger felt that they should celebrate their escape. It was easier to find an explanation for the part played by the bamboo charm. When nearly all Japanese houses had thatched roofs, any fire was liable to spread to neighbouring houses. So, whenever a fire broke out, people climbed on the nearby roofs and tried to sweep off all sparks or burning fragments with brooms. When thatch was replaced by tiles, in urban or suburban houses, that particular danger became less pressing, but the once utilitarian broom survived in symbolic form.

Appointment in Japan

Despite the threats of natural disaster, Japan in the 1920s provided the visitor with an unusual combination of the picturesque and the sedate and orderly. Orderliness at that time I took for granted. I did not realise what a rare quality it was subsequently to become in many parts of the world. The stranger could then wander through the streets by night as by day, without the least anxiety. I remember meeting the train of a friend of mine who arrived at Nagoya station at 2 A.M. I walked three or four miles from my house through the thoroughfares and byways of a quiet, deserted city. It never occurred to me that there was any danger of molestation, nor was there. In this respect, despite all the changes of the last half-century, Japan can still claim to be superior to most other countries.

The most common inconvenience suffered by the Westerner in provincial towns, where he was a rarity, arose from the curiosity which his size, dress, complexion and demeanour excited. Groups of Japanese, mainly children, were liable to gather round foreigners and make comments on their oddity. In out-of-the-way places the traffic would stop and cyclists dismount to get a better view. If a foreigner entered a shop, a few people were likely to follow and watch him making a purchase. They usually shied away if he made approaches to them and soon dispersed if he addressed them. One's fellow-passenger in a train or tramcar would often put the customary questions, "Where are you going? What country have you come from? What is your business? How many children have you?"

It was foolish to show annoyance at these attentions, which were attributable simply to amiable curiosity. At least I was never conscious of any hostility towards me among the crowds. The only time when I sensed that some Japanese might not be as well disposed towards Westerners as they appeared to be was during the passage through Congress of the United States' Immigration Act, which struck a damaging blow at the nation's pride. By now this Act has been forgotten, except by historians. At the time, however, it had a significant effect on international relations, and so deserves comment.

During the early and middle years of the *Meiji* era, large numbers of Japanese had emigrated to Hawaii and California, but by the first decade of the present century, restrictions on all emigrants from Asia had been imposed by the United States government. There was some discrimination in Japan's favour, and from 1907 onwards, under a gentleman's agreement, she had been permitted to continue to send 250 emigrants a year to California. Thus Japan could feel that she was not classed with other Asian countries whose people were completely excluded. In 1924, however, Congress passed the Immigration Act which shut out Japanese entirely and so removed the distinction. This action awakened indignation throughout the country. Japan had become one of the Great Powers, yet her people were treated as if they belonged to one of the lesser breeds. Some writers and speakers urged that, in retaliation, American missionaries should be expelled from Japan on the grounds that the country that sent them had no real understanding of Christian principles. An irate journalist applied to Americans the words that Clemenceau applied to President Wilson: "They talk like Jesus Christ and act like Lloyd George." Sun Yat-Sen, the revolutionary Chinese leader, was visiting Japan at the time and his welcome was all the warmer because it could be made the occasion for supporting his advocacy of an Asian Federation to confuse Western, especially American, imperialism. A patriot tried to underline the national protest by disembowelling himself outside the offices of the Standard Oil Company, mistaking it for the American Embassy. The Japanese people were far too well-mannered to vent their wrath on individual foreign residents, but occasionally, when I passed groups of school-children in the village, they called out: "*Amerikajin baka*" (American fool). So I was able to infer the conversation among their parents that went on behind the *shoji*. On the face of it, the Immigration

Appointment in Japan

Act was of little practical importance. Nonetheless, it affected the mood of the Japanese towards the West and may have played its part in the nationalism of the subsequent years.

IV

Students and Teachers

As I explained in the opening chapter, the government College to which I had been appointed was known as a *Koto Shogyo Gakko*, or Commercial High School, and was the equivalent of the continental Handelshochschule, on which it and similar foundations had been modelled. They resembled fairly closely the Faculties of Commerce in British universities, and during the period of their existence, they played an important part in training men for business careers. Many of the old students whom I have met on subsequent visits to Japan went on to occupy leading posts in banking, industry and commerce. With the changes in the educational system that were introduced under American guidance after the Second World War, all these colleges disappeared. The Nagoya *Koto Shogyo Gakko* became the Faculty of Economics in the new University of Nagoya.

The students, who came from the middle schools at the age of seventeen, normally remained at the College for three years. The oldest of them were not far short of my own age, which I kept as dark as possible. While the majority of those who graduated entered business life, a few went on to university, chiefly to the University of Commerce in Tokyo, now Hitotsubashi University. These students usually followed academic careers. The College recruited 180–200 new entrants every year, so that its full complement, when it had been in existence for three years, approached 600.

The College building was a two-storey wooden structure

Appointment in Japan

to which a large assembly hall built of concrete was added a year after my arrival. There were dormitories in which many of the students lived, and extensive sports grounds with open country beyond. To reach the College from my house I had, at first, a pleasant walk through farmland, but, towards the end of my time, some of this was swallowed up by the advancing suburbs.

The College possessed a remarkably good library of works on economics and general literature both in Japanese and in European languages. The furnishings and equipment of lecture rooms and staff rooms were austere but adequate. The students wore dark-blue uniforms and peaked caps with the College emblem. The uniforms gave them a military appearance, but this impression, which most foreigners carried away with them, was deceptive. To the Japanese, the advantage of the uniforms was that they were cheap, and that they discouraged ostentation by the well-to-do students. The dress and the practice of wearing the hair closely cropped were in accord with the tradition of austerity which modern Japan had taken over from her feudal elite, the *Samurai*.

Some students, in their anxiety to avoid ostentation, cultivated a practice of extreme shabbiness. Torn and tattered uniforms became a mark of their status. In the evenings, however, especially in summer, the uniforms were often discarded in favour of Japanese dress. This transformed the appearance and, it seemed to me, the personalities of the students. On one occasion the uniforms were doffed without being replaced. This happened when the students on their way from their dormitories and lodgings were caught in a sudden storm and arrived at the lecture room drenched to the skin. They sensibly took off all their clothes and, when I entered the lecture room, I was faced with an audience completely naked except for the cushions which had been transferred from seats to laps. I suppose that I was taken aback at this unusual sight, for the students who knew something about Western conventions showed their enjoyment at my evident, if momentary,

Students and Teachers

discomfiture. However, by this time I had learnt to accept any new experience as it occurred, and I proceeded with my lecture without comment.

For their mid-day meal most of the students had cold boiled rice, pickles and tea. On this meagre diet they worked very hard and were subjected to a formidable programme of lectures which were the main method of instruction. The teaching day began at 8 A.M. in the summer and at 8.30 A.M. in the winter. It was, I suppose an example of educational mass-production which is inevitable when large numbers are involved, and there were few opportunities for individual tuition. Nevertheless, individuality and personal taste found ample expression in extra-curricular activities. In a sense, these were the epitome of Japanese life, for they included traditional games, sports and artistic activities as well as those imported from the West. The traditional sports included *judo* and *sumo* (both forms of wrestling), *kendo* (fencing) and archery, but many students preferred football, baseball or tennis.

Musical societies existed for the practice of both Japanese and European music. Some played the *shakuhachi* or recited *nagauta* (ballads); others played classical and modern music on Western instruments, among which the harmonica was one of the most popular. Many of them were keenly interested in drama, and they gave performances of both Japanese and Western plays. I remember a performance of Maeterlinck's *Bluebird* in French; a play advertised as *Tsuki no De* turned out to be Lady Gregory's *The Rising of the Moon*. An even more ambitious venture was a multilingual allegory on international relations written by a member of the College staff.

I was always impressed when the students were performing a scene from some old Japanese play. In assuming not only the dress but the demeanour of the heroes of the past, they seemed to rise to a different plane of existence from that which they normally inhabited. Whenever I witnessed this apparent transformation in manners and character, I was persuaded that, whatever the surface changes in the country, the current of traditional sentiment was still flowing strongly.

Where Japanese student activities differed most from those of their Western counterparts was in the absence of political societies, equivalent to the Conservative, Liberal or Labour Clubs of most British universities. Japanese students were by no means indifferent to politics, and international questions aroused keen interest among them. Yet the political system at that time, though modelled on Western parliamentary institutions, provided few opportunities for popular participation in policy-making. Parliamentary government did not mean democratic government. Power was transmitted downwards from the Emperor and his advisers. The political parties were not based on differences in political principles. They could scarcely be said even to represent different interests and the predominant party did not control the executive. Thus there was little inducement for the students to form political clubs associated with the parties, and I do not remember that a meeting of a political character was ever held in the College in my time.

The absence of overt political activity did not mean that the students were docile before authority. On the contrary, they often expressed their disapproval of their teachers or of educational policy, and they sometimes asserted their opinions in ways that were then quite shocking to one brought up in the English tradition. In Britain the days of student unrest, violence on the campus (the latter then a meaningless term to Englishmen), and the demands for student participation in the running of academic institutions, were undreamt of. In Japan, however, they had already arrived. Although the teaching staff was normally treated with far greater deference by the pupils than was customary in the West, the College authorities became easily alarmed at any manifestation of student displeasure. The tenure of unpopular teachers was insecure, and students were sometimes ruthless in expressing their dissatisfaction. In notes written soon after I took up my appointment at the College I recorded that the authorities seemed frightened of the student body and that they could not be relied upon to back up teachers against protesting students even in circumstances in which the former were not obviously at fault. I have already mentioned my amusement when I was told by the Principal at the outset of my career at Nagoya that above all else I must please the students. I found, though, that in telling me this he was simply expressing an accepted pedagogic principle.

On a certain graduation day at Nagoya, when some of the senior students were called upon to make what were expected to be formal ceremonial speeches, they launched out on a bitter criticism of the College, its curriculum and its methods of instruction. Even in the middle schools, strikes for the removal of unpopular teachers were not uncommon. At Waseda University, one of the great private universities, the students revolted against the introduction of military studies. At Nagoya where, since it was a government College, time was assigned for what we should call cadet corps exercises, the officer in charge was greeted with disdain by many of the students. This was not because of any personal fault of character, for he was a charming and modest person, but simply because of his profession. The time of which I am writing is regarded as a liberal period in Japanese political history. The defeat of the Central Powers by the parliamentary democracies of Britain, France and the United States had strengthened the influence of Japanese who favoured free institutions and representative government. Hitherto, under the Constitution introduced in 1890, the Emperor had exercised his prerogative on the advice of Ministers who composed the Cabinet. These Ministers were not responsible to parliament but to the Emperor alone, and in choosing a Prime Minister the Emperor acted on the advice of a body of elder statesmen (*genro*). Parliamentary interference in the field of defence was completely excluded, and in foreign relations the main organ of advice was the Privy Council, which was quite independent of parliamentary control. Finally, the financial authority of parliament was limited by a constitutional provision that, should it fail to pass the budget, the government could proceed with the budget of the previous year. All these autocratic or paternalistic features of the government came under adverse criticism after the First World War, partly for the reasons already indicated. Outbreaks of popular disapproval, such as the celebrated Rice Riots of 1918, disturbed the complacency of the ruling cliques and the *genro* realised that concessions had to be made. For the first time in Japanese history, the leader of a political party was chosen as Prime Minister, and it seemed possible that the age of parliamentary government was about to begin. Although the cause of the progressives received a setback with the murder of Prime Minister Hara in 1921, a few years later parliamentary influence was re-established when another politician became Prime Minister. The triumphant moment came in 1925 with the passing of the Manhood Suffrage Act. The students as a body were whole-hearted supporters of these trends, and they did not hesitate to make their views known. Their protests against authority, however, were themselves usually limited, so far as I could tell, to parochial matters and were directed against some specific fault, real or imagined in the educational system. There was no revolutionary purpose behind the protests.

At the time I explained the phenomenon to myself by a complacent reference to Japan's political immaturity and to the impact of institutional arrangements, imported from the West, on the traditional way of life. No coherent political initiative could be expected from the mass of the people nursed in an authoritarian tradition. The expression of discontent and criticism thus devolved on the privileged student class as the most independent, sophisticated and articulate group in society. One of the most obvious objects of its attack was the educational system itself. It did not occur to me that the same unruly behaviour was ever likely to be seen in Britain where, as I said at the time, students as a body were probably just as conservative as their elders.

Students and Teachers

It may give some comfort to those who are disturbed by the behaviour and manners of students today to learn that in Japan the generation that passed through the colleges in the 1920s, and are now elderly men, look back on their student days with nostalgia and gratitude. They are active supporters of their alumni associations and never lose an opportunity of expressing their obligations to their old teachers, for whom they have a warm regard. I have attended their parties and meetings, which are sentimental occasions for recalling the pleasures of their college days and end with the singing of the College Song. The fiftieth and sixtieth anniversaries of the founding of the Nagoya *Koto Shogyo Gakko* were celebrated with much pomp and circumstance. A commemorative volume which contains a record of the College's history and of all its teachers and graduates has been published and has been dispatched to all past members of the College both in Japan and in the most distant parts of the world.

The graduates have thus long forgotten their old discontents. Most of them, it must be admitted, have become successful business and professional men, having risen on the tide of Japan's economic expansion – a growth to which they themselves have contributed. Worldly success, however, is not the only source of the strong attachment they have for their old College. Japanese life is pervaded by its group loyalties and by a powerful sense of reciprocal obligation. Once a man has received a benefit from another, he cannot avoid making some return, however irksome this obligation may be. The student incurs a debt to his teacher which remains throughout his life. Although my period of service in the College was short (only two and a half years), old students extend most generous hospitality to me whenever I visit Japan and I have been touched by the repeated kindnesses of the various branches of the alumni society, which is now composed largely of students who passed through the College long after I left.

On the other side, it must be said that Japanese teachers were expected to maintain high standards both in their academic and in their private life. The Confucian tradition which required them to be superior to the commonalty doubtless moulded their conduct. In spite of the troubles that occurred from time to time, the students were disposed to treat them with respect and, although there were some humbugs and pedants in their ranks, they were in the main devoted and conscientious men whose responsibilities for their pupils extended far beyond those normally accepted by their counterparts in Britain.

These responsibilities sometimes imposed an excessively heavy burden on particular teachers. The Dean of a University Faculty once enumerated to an English colleague and myself all the obligations that he had to fulfil towards his students, both while they were within the university precincts and also during vacations. "For instance," he said, "last vacation, just as I was about to take a holiday, I heard that one of the students in my Faculty had been injured in a mountaineering accident. I had to abandon my plans and go to him." Then he asked: "What would an English Dean have done if he had heard that one of the students in his Faculty had fallen down a precipice in the Alps?" We felt obliged to tell him that, so far as the English Dean was concerned, the student would probably have been left there!

The devotion of teachers to their pupils' welfare was recognised by their fellow-countrymen. This was probably one reason why the teacher, ill-paid as he was, enjoyed a high repute. An experience provided me with an illustration of the respect in which teachers were held. A man sitting next to me in a tramcar got into conversation with me and proceeded to ask the usual questions about where I was going and where I had come from. When I had answered these to his satisfaction, he asked: "Are you with Mitsubishi?" "No," I replied, "I am teaching at the *Koto Shogyo Gakko*." At this, he rose in his seat, raised his hat, bowed, and acknowledged my communication in a tone of utmost respect. I much enjoyed recounting this experience to British friends who were engineers on the staff of the Mitsubishi Company!

Students and Teachers

Most of the higher educational institutions employed a few foreigners, the majority of whom were engaged in teaching languages. At the Nagoya *Koto Shogyo Gakko* in my day there were two Englishmen, a Canadian, an American sports instructor, a German, a Chinese and a Russian lady. We were called upon by our Japanese colleagues for explanations whenever they met with difficulties in their reading, no matter what the subject. I am afraid that my range of scholarship, or the fertility of my imagination, was not always equal to the demands. However, I did my best, as I found that a confession of ignorance about any aspect of European civilisation evoked surprise, and even mild disapproval.

Colloquialisms encountered in contemporary English literature or drama were naturally puzzling to Japanese readers. "I cannot find this word in the dictionary," complained a Professor of English to me. The word was "Abso-bloody-lutely". Stage directions in a Galsworthy play (Galsworthy was a popular author at that time among the Japanese) raised grave suspicions in his mind. In one of the scenes, a young man had put his arm around a young woman. She disengaged herself, but when he persisted the stage directions stated: "So she yielded the point." "What point did she yield?" asked the Professor nervously.

The routine of teaching was constantly being punctuated by episodes of this kind. Not all the mistakes were on one side. Fortunately, my colleagues were for the most part men of lively humour, and we enjoyed our mutual linguistic misunderstandings. One of my foreign colleagues, fluent in colloquial Japanese, announced to us all in that language that his wife was coming from Europe to join him, and that he was making arrangements for her arrival. His announcement gave his Japanese audience some hilarious moments, as they later told me. He had used the honorific term *okusan* when referring to his wife instead of the derogatory term *kanai* (equivalent to "my wife"). The Japanese knew what he meant – but what he had actually said was that someone else's wife was joining him!

Appointment in Japan

Although foreign teachers were expected to be versatile, most Japanese teachers in universities and higher educational institutions, particularly in economics, were very highly specialised. Today, with the development of the subject, specialisation has much increased among British university teachers, but at that time it was unusual, and the limitation of range which the Japanese gladly accepted surprised me. I once tried to discuss with an eminent Japanese economic historian, who had specialised in British economic history, certain analogies with the economic development of his own country. He declared himself to be unable to help, saying that Japanese economic history was not one of his interests. Theorists were much less ready than their counterparts in Britain in those days, to venture into the applied field. Although Marxism seemed to have great attractions in the inter-war years for economists and economic historians, the recent progress in the Japanese economy, which, to put it mildly, is not readily explained by Marxist doctrine, has dimmed their enthusiasm. There are few Japanese today who would think of asking the sort of question put to a leading British economist early in the post-war period: "From the standpoint of my academic career, would it be better for me to become a Marxist or a Keynesian?" Even at that time he was not, of course, typical. Nowadays the outlook and training of Japanese academics are well attuned to those of their Western colleagues, and in most fields the Japanese have made notable contributions. In economics this is certainly true. In particular, their work in mathematical economic theory has won them a distinguished international reputation. Perhaps their acknowledged success in that branch of the subject can be explained by the fact that it is easier to communicate with foreigners in mathematical symbols than in ordinary language.

The inclination of pre-war academics toward Marxism had some unforeseen consequences. A contemporary economist who takes a jaundiced view of the usefulness of his professional colleagues as advisers on policy asserted, paradoxically, that his country owes some of its recent success to the fact that at the time when Japan emerged from the War, most of the serious academic economists were Marxists. Since the post-war government was not disposed to turn to them for advice, it had to fall back on bureaucrats and administrators whose economics had been learnt mainly by experience. Some of these were engineers by training and their instinct was to find a solution for post-war problems in enhanced technical efficiency and innovation rather than in the management of demand. So, according to this economist, Japan escaped the neo-Keynesian blight which afflicted Western countries. While this assertion must not be taken literally, it does have a certain validity.

An episode in the 1930s showed me that even Marxism had a Japanese complexion. A distinguished economist from Tokyo, who had once been a colleague, recounted an experience which had left him shocked. While he was in London, he considered it his duty to visit Karl Marx's grave and to pay his respects. When he enquired of a passer-by the location of Highgate Cemetery, and explained the reason for wanting to know, he found that this Londoner had never even heard of Karl Marx. When, at last, he found the grave, he was horrified to see that it was in a badly neglected condition. To him there was nothing inconsistent in revolutionary doctrine and ancestor-worship.

The students at the *Koto Shogyo Gakko*, though mainly concerned with economics and business subjects, received a good general education. English studies occupied much of their time. Through these they gained some acquaintance with modern literature as well as with the writings of Western economists. Sometimes the choice of authors for study surprised me. Ruskin, Stevenson, Galsworthy, Shaw and Ibsen – a queer mixture. From time to time English-speaking contests (otherwise called oratorical contests) were held at which candidates from various higher educational institutions in the neighbourhood competed. The speeches were judged by a panel of foreign and Japanese teachers. The contests were popular and were always attended by a large audience of both students and adults. The candidates, with the help of their teachers, prepared papers on a wide variety of subjects and spent weeks in rehearsing their delivery. These occasions brought out several aspects of the Japanese character which were new to me. First, they demonstrated the pertinacity and seriousness of young Japanese men and women in their search for new knowledge and aptitudes. The students did not spare themselves in their efforts to become proficient. They were determined to excel. Second, I admired the ease with which young men and girls comported themselves when faced by a large and critical audience. They were able to conquer their usual shyness and spoke out boldly.

The contests also made me realise the remarkable capacity of the Japanese to endure boredom without giving overt evidence of their suffering. The speeches went on hour after lengthening hour, and still the audience, many of whom probably understood little of what was being said, sat in apparently happy appreciation. However, the contests also revealed to me what seemed to a Western observer to be less admirable qualities. For instance, on one occasion the first prize was awarded to a competitor from a neighbouring Girls' High School. The male students were furious, partly because their dignity was affronted by the judges' decision in favour of one of the weaker sex, and partly because the subject – Be Kind to Animals – was so infantile in its intellectual content compared with their own lofty contributions on public affairs and morals.

In another contest, my suggestion that a certain student should be chosen to represent our College, because his spoken English was far superior to that of anyone else, was turned down by my colleagues on the grounds that he was only in his second year. The third-year students would have been affronted if a second-year student were preferred to any of them. In the event a contestant was chosen who did badly. His failure had an outcome which also threw an unflattering light on Japanese sportsmanship. When the question of the College's participation in the next contest arose, the Principal laid down that we must not send in a candidate unless we were certain to win. He obviously had no use for any such nonsense as counting the game more than the prize.

The episode provides an example, admittedly a trivial one, of the importance which the Japanese attach to success. No doubt, their perseverance and determination to excel account for much of their massive achievement since that time. In the 1920s, though inwardly convinced of their superiority to other people, they knew that this fact was not acknowledged outside Japan. So they were inclined to take offence easily at any slight, and they considered failure a disgrace. It seems to me that through their recognised and undeniable successes during the last forty years, they have acquired confidence and a sound sense of proportion.

My association with these contests brought me further insight into Japanese attitudes. The candidates were supposed to compose their own speeches, with the help of their tutors. My faith in the authenticity of the contributions was, however, shaken when I heard one of them offering as his own work an article (unsigned) which I had myself written for the *Japan Chronicle*! When I expostulated with a Japanese professor who had taken the chair at the meeting, he was quite unmoved and gave me to understand that plagiarism was a common practice among the contestants. Later, at the time of the entrance examinations, one of my Japanese colleagues was dismayed because I had given a low mark to a particular candidate. "We cannot send in a mark like this," he said, "he is the son of X" (a prominent personage). At the time this episode shocked me. Further reflection, however, leads me to suppose that although in Britain it would have been unthinkable to suggest to an examiner that he should alter his marks for such a reason, some college authorities might nevertheless have offered the privileged candidate a place.

Although at the beginning of my career at Nagoya I found difficulty in distinguishing one student from another, partly because of the uniformity of their attire, many of them soon revealed a strongly-marked individuality. Most of them were interested in their foreign teachers and some were tireless in their efforts to help us. The more earnest among them used to call at my house, where they could practise their English. I enjoyed their society and learned much from them. While they were critical of some aspects of the College, they conformed to the rules, and few failed to stay the course. I remember only two who did not do so. One, a gruff, humorous and likeable lad, took to drink. He was sent down and went to expiate his faults by several years of hard manual labour. He seemed to bear no resentment for this treatment and I was told that, after this interval, he returned to the College and graduated without difficulty. Another rejected the business career for which he was being prepared. Instead of answering the examination paper which I had set, he handed in an essay in which he affirmed, in terms that I found quite moving, his intention to abandon his studies and to devote himself to a religious life.

In the 1920s the American film exerted an enormous influence in those parts of the world where old ways of life were being discarded. It was taken very seriously by students. The local cinemas showed chiefly the silliest and most tedious of the Hollywood products. Yet the students were keen patrons because they hoped to improve their knowledge of Western ways of living. They often urged me to accompany them so that I could explain any obscurities. Occasionally I accepted their invitations, but I often took evasive action as I could not always endure the five or six hours of banality which was the normal length of a cinema show. As a direct refusal would have been offensive, I had to find a plausible excuse on these occasions.

My acquaintance with Japanese education in the 1920s led me to suppose that, while it had faults, it was decidedly more egalitarian than the British system. This conclusion I elaborated in my first book on Japan, written soon after my return to England. There was no equivalent of our private system of preparatory and public schools. Almost all children went to the state primary schools, and places in the higher schools and universities were allotted mainly as a result of competitive examinations among many candidates. I was only too well aware of the last point, since every spring my colleagues and I were faced with the task of marking well over a thousand scripts from applicants for admission to the *Koto Shogyo Gakko*.

The British practice of providing an expensive privileged education for the few who could expect to become leaders in public affairs appealed to Japanese of traditional mould, and some harboured a romantic notion of our public schools. The more liberal-minded, however, regarded the British system less favourably. These views were conveyed to me by such questions as: "I have been told that poor boys are not allowed to go to your best schools or to Oxford and Cambridge. Is this true?". In the late 1960s, a senior executive of a great Japanese business house, who had spent some years in London, mentioned the surprise he felt as it dawned on him that a very high proportion of the leading positions in the City, politics and the Civil Service were held, in an allegedly socialist-governed Britain, by a small group who had been educated at a few privileged schools. He found that even in large-scale industry, where the sources of enterprise, inventive genius and administrative capacity of the highest quality are varied and unsignposted, authority was still often vested in people with the same educational experience. On all this our candid Japanese friend cast a half-admiring eye. At the same time, he wondered whether the narrow educational basis of British leadership might provide part of the explanation for Britain's stagnant economy and for the divisions in our society.

Later reflection and more extensive knowledge of Japan led me to modify my original views on the degree of egalitarianism. I was right in thinking that in Japan the path to success in the professions, the Civil Service and finance was open to persons of more diverse social origins than in Britain. Nevertheless, I had neglected to observe the extent to which leadership in public affairs, the law and the higher reaches of private enterprise rested, in fact, in the hands of those who had been trained in particular types of schools. These were the *Koto Gakko* (High Schools) which provided a mainly literary education for pupils between the ages of seventeen and twenty and from which the various departments of the five Imperial Universities were largely recruited. The most famous of these schools was the *Dai Ichi Koto Gakko* (the First Higher School) of Tokyo. I was well acquainted with the *Dai Hachi Koto Gakko* (the Eighth Higher School), for I lived within a stone's throw of it at Nagoya and I numbered some of its teachers among my friends.

Before the Second World War, civil servants, business and professional people – the men trained in those schools – had to share authority with the military. After the War the influence of the *Koto Gakko* alumni reached its apogee. Public policy and public administration were dominated by them. They formed a cohesive group which supplied the self-confidence and capable leadership called for at that period of confusion. From this, one might conclude that Japan's educational system in its higher reaches and the impact that the system made upon the country's administration was broadly similar to Britain's. This conclusion would be a half-truth. Alongside these schools, and the arts and legal faculties of the Imperial Universities, there was a wide range of schools, colleges and universities designed to provide scientific, technical and commercial education for those intent upon careers in industry and commerce. Some of these were state institutions, like the *Koto Shogyo Gakko*, others were private. From early in the *Meiji* era, certain prominent business houses established links with colleges and universities that might provide recruits for managerial and technical posts. It was said that the great Mitsubishi concern was built on the founder's money and men from Keio University. Through institutions of this kind, Japan equipped herself to absorb quickly the expert knowledge that the West had to offer and her industrial progress owed much to that capacity.

Although in my first years in Japan I was only dimly aware of the wide range of Japan's educational system, the practical effects soon forced themselves on my attention. As an economist interested in industrial affairs, I took any opportunities offered of meeting businessmen and company officials. In my first book on Japan, *Modern Japan and its Problems*, written in 1927, I recorded my surprise at finding that most of the officials of the large industrial companies, banks and merchant houses, and not only those employed by large concerns, had received some kind of professional training of a university standard, including that provided by the *Koto Gogyo Gakko* (Technical High Schools), *Koto Shogyo Gakko*, or by universities specialising in engineering, economics or allied subjects.

A few years ago I had the opportunity of seeing a list of the graduates of Nagoya *Koto Shogyo Gakko* and of their occupations. The roll of alumni in high managerial or administrative posts was very impressive. During my several visits to Japan I have always met a number of old students who have taken their place among the leaders of the country's industrial, financial and commercial life.

The Nagoya College was not unique. Indeed, a college for business education had been established in Tokyo as long ago as 1875. Initially it was a private foundation but it was later taken over by the government and has since developed into the Hitotsubashi University. Several other institutions of the same type can trace their origins back to the beginning of this century, and by the 1930s there were eleven *Koto Shogyo Gakko* as well as three government universities which specialised in economics and commercial studies. Between them, these institutions and other universities with economics departments probably produced at least three thousand graduates a year. This was at a time when only a few hundred students graduated annually in these subjects at British universities.

The effect on the quality of the business executives was

marked. Whereas in Japan a large proportion of them had received a higher education of a specialised or professional character, in Britain the majority of managerial or administrative posts were still filled by people with a general education or no higher education at all. Much of British industry was in the hands of self-made men who had worked their way up or of those who owed their position to nepotism. Some experiences a few years after I left Japan in 1925 brought out very clearly the contrast in intellectual quality between the typical Japanese executive or manager and his British counterpart. In the late 1920s I was engaged on a study of the West Midlands industries. I found that one of my chief problems was that of explaining to businessmen from whom I was trying to collect information the nature of scientific economic enquiry. As many of them had had no contact with the academic world, they had some difficulty in understanding why anyone outside their trade should have any interest in the development of their firms or the organisation of their industry. In the mid-1930s, when I was conducting a rather similar enquiry among Japanese businessmen, I met with no such scepticism or bewilderment. Their educational experience enabled them to appreciate the nature of scientific enquiry and the language in which its communications were made.

Since that time there have been immense changes. The British businessman is now only too keenly aware of the interest taken by outsiders in his activities. He spends hours of his frustrated life filling in official or academic questionnaires. The big companies, which were once reluctant to recruit administrative staff from the universities, now compete with one another for the services of graduates. Nonetheless, in this respect British business is about two generations behind the Japanese.

The fault is not to be ascribed only, or even mainly, to the conservatism of the business world. The British educational system must bear most of the blame. Neither the public schools nor Oxford and Cambridge regarded careers in industry and commerce as worthy of their best pupils.

Students and Teachers

For a very long time technical and vocational studies were despised, and even science was neglected. In Japan their practical worth was recognised in the early days of her modernisation, and large numbers of the most able students were attracted to technological studies, especially engineering. Both countries directed much of their education resources to the production of an elite. The difference between them was that Japan's elite was trained to handle the technological and administrative problems of the twentieth century, whereas Britain's elite, through its educational experience, was ill-equipped for leadership in a modern industrial society.

During the Occupation after the Second World War, the whole Japanese educational system was reorganised on American lines. The new system provided for six years of primary school, three years of Junior High School, three years of Senior High School, and four years of university or college. From the beginning of the present century, practically all boys and girls had attended primary schools, but now the opportunities for secondary and higher education were greatly increased. The majority now have the benefit of secondary education up to the age of eighteen, and about a third of those between the ages of eighteen and twenty-two are able to attend universities or colleges of higher education. The admirers of the old system are distressed at what they regard as a decline in the quality of education, yet few found it expedient to oppose the wide extension of education to the mass of the people. Since the places in secondary schools and universities are filled by competitive examination, the conclusion might be drawn that opportunities for academic success are available to all able pupils irrespective of the wealth or social standing of their families. But this conclusion would be a half-truth. In fact, at the higher levels of education, the dice is heavily loaded in favour of the already well-to-do.

The entrance examinations are of crucial importance, and parents who are well-off can afford to have their

Appointment in Japan

children coached for the examinations set by the most reputable secondary schools. Once admitted, a child stands a much better chance of getting into one of the universities of high standing, especially if he has had the benefit of additional skilled coaching. The educational advantages of having well-to-do parents do not end here. The fees charged by the state university are low and grants are available to poor students who attend them. However, if a poor student fails to get admission he has no other recourse, for the fees charged by the private universities are very high. Places in the latter, therefore, are filled largely by children of the well-to-do. A few of these private universities, such as Keio, are among the best. It seems evident that, with the increase in the size of universities and in the number of students, the gap between the standards of the best and of the others has been widening. The institutions of second rank are extremely overcrowded and understaffed, and the conditions in some of them may have been a leading cause of student disorders.

Success in an academic career is especially important in Japan, since not only the professions but also business concerns look to the universities to provide them with trained recruits. The strength of group loyalties in Japan means that those who have been at college together are linked for life in a tacit mutual assistance association, and those who have graduated from the most reputable universities have the best chance of success in their careers. Thus, while there remains some justification for my conclusion of sixty years ago, that Japan's social cohesion and her strong sense of common purpose have been fostered by the absence of a divisive educational system, egalitarianism in higher education is illusory.

In recent years many Japanese have become highly critical of the competitive entrance examinations. They argue that the examinations impose an excessive strain on the candidates who, once admitted to the institutions of their choice, feel assured of a privileged position in the market for good jobs and see no reason to exert themselves during the rest of their academic career. While this argument has doubtless been pitched too strongly, it cannot be disregarded.

V

How Others See Us

I had not been in Japan long before I realised the immense possibilities of misunderstanding that existed whenever a Japanese had dealings with a Westerner, or when the Japanese government was negotiating with those of the Western world. To the more obvious difficulties raised by linguistic barriers, there were added the sources of misunderstanding that came from the differences in tradition and stages of economic development. In the early 1920s, though acknowledged as one of the Great Powers by virtue of her military and naval strength, Japan was much poorer than any Western or Central European country and her modern industry was still narrowly limited in its range. Those foreign visitors to, or residents in, the country who had little appreciation of the perspective of history were liable to pass unfavourable judgements both on the quality of the country's civilisation and on the practical capacity of its inhabitants. A few examples may illustrate my point.

In those days it was commonly held by the foreign business community that the Japanese, despite their skill as craftsmen, were incompetent as technicians. It was said that they had no mechanical sense, that they were brutal in their treatment of delicate apparatus, and that they lacked sensitivity and judgement as drivers of cars or as pilots of aeroplanes. Sir George Sansom, in *The Western World and Japan*, had noted a similar attitude among foreigners in early *Meiji* times. Only persons of Western origin, it was then assumed, were capable of manipulating valves and levers.

The success of the Japanese in all branches of engineering has long silenced these criticisms. The fact is that natural capacity had little to do with the deficiencies found by the Europeans. Half a century ago Japan was only on the threshold of modern technology, and few Japanese had much experience of the gadgets and mechanical devices already widely used in the West. They were, however, quick to overtake their mentors, and this did not surprise me. Just before I left for Japan I had spent some months in investigating the eighteenth-century firm of Boulton and Watt, renowned for the manufacture and installation of the new steam engine. The firm's papers were full of complaints about the incompetence of those who supplied components and about the ineptitude of users of the engines. Cylinder castings ordered from the local foundries were liable to be an inch or more too small for the pistons, or so much larger than specification that the pistons had to be packed with leather when the engine was assembled. My British friends were not impressed with the analogies which I drew between Britain in the late eighteenth century and Japan in the early twentieth century. Nevertheless, subsequent history has shown that Japan was then at the point which British engineering had reached long ago.

The complacency of Westerners, so confident of their inherently superior gifts for technology, must have been a constant irritant to their Japanese business acquaintances. During my voyage out, a young representative of a Lancashire cotton firm informed me that Japan's recent successes in the Eastern textile markets were simply attributable to the circumstances of the War, and that the inherited skill and experience of Lancashire would soon re-establish British supremacy.

Failure to view Japanese institutions in historical perspective was responsible for many misunderstandings in the political and social, as well as in the economic, sphere. The British and the Americans were inclined to accept at their face value Japan's own affirmations of the peculiarities of her civilisation. Of course, every civilisation has unique features, and Japan presented some striking contrasts to the Western world of the twentieth century. Yet it was not difficult to detect many analogies between modern Japan and ancient or mediaeval Europe.

A knowledge of classical history was probably as good a foundation as any for a Westerner who wanted to understand the nature of Japan's civilisation and to sympathise with the outlook of her people. I read Alfred Zimmern's *The Greek Commonwealth* in my second year in Japan. I found the analogies drawn between the ancient Greeks and the modern Japanese exciting and illuminating. Pericles' proud boast, "We are lovers of beauty without extravagance", might have been made by the Japanese, whose superb aesthetic tradition was still alive. The Shinto deities (*kami*) bore a close resemblance to the members of the Greek or Roman pantheon, a question I discussed only a few years ago with a Japanese professor of Greek. The chief difference, he pointed out, was that Shinto was not associated with any tradition of blood sacrifice, at any rate not since the influence of Buddhism began to prevail in Japan. The Shinto gods are not ill-tempered, jealous and thin-skinned deities whose wrath has to be appeased by sacrifices, such as those of Iphigenia or Isaac; they are, for the most part, genial gods that are pleasant to have around. The Shinto shrines, whether presiding over waterfalls, rocks and places of natural beauty, or factories, offices, schools and households, are comforting and friendly.

Misunderstandings about the attitude of the Japanese to their Emperor, their country and their great men might have been avoided if these analogies with the ancient world had been in the minds of European commentators. Indeed, there were remarkable similarities between the politico-religious developments in Rome in the early days of the Principate and those in the *Meiji* era. Ancient religious sentiments and myths were deliberately revived to fortify the state and to increase the veneration for its dead. In *Meiji* Japan, as in Augustine Rome, the national shrines were rebuilt and became the focus of patriotic fervour. In both countries divine attributes were ascribed to the Emperor. Although in the past the Emperor of Japan had been treated with scant regard by powerful subjects, by the time the *Meiji* nation-builders had done their work, he had moved into the company of the gods.

Any slighting reference to him, or even a suggestion that did not accord with the principle that he was the source of all political authority, brought punishment to the offender. While I was in Japan a well-known professor of law, Professor Minobe, had propounded a theory that the Emperor was to be revered, not as the fount of all authority, but rather as an organ of the state. There was an outcry at his irreverence and he was dismissed from his Chair. A high official in one of the great business houses told me solemnly that, whereas in the West, law was made by the peoples' parliamentary representatives, in Japan it was handed down from the Emperor and for that reason had greater sanctity. This, he thought, was an instance of Japan's essential superiority to the West. He was not at all pleased when I tactlessly pointed out that the idea of a divine lawgiver was common to most civilisations in their early stages. In the same way, many constitutional practices which were thought strange by those who had come from countries with democratic parliamentary institutions, were very similar to the practices of states where power was or had been vested in a monarchy or an aristocracy. It was easy to find examples from history or from the modern world of countries where the leading ministers were not responsible to parliament and where the military leaders had a dominant role in the determination of policy.

It pleased me at the time to look for these similarities. I had to be careful in talking about them to the Japanese, however, for I found that while some listened to my views with interest and even amusement, others were affronted. The analogies with the ancient world pleased me most. Nevertheless, on the occasions when I was a spectator at pageants or religious processions, I could imagine myself to be in mediaeval Europe. Then, when I looked into Japan's modern industry and met some of her business leaders, my mind turned rather to Samuel Smiles and his enterprising, hardworking and frugal heroes. Or, when I got to know something of the great widely ramified business houses, the *Zaibatsu*, I thought of the Fuggers of Augsberg. There were also some examples of the type of business leader referred to by the mocking donor of a copy of Fox Bourne's *English Merchants*, which came into my possession a few years ago. On the fly-leaf there was inscribed: "For Malcolm; may the history of these enterprising, charitable and capable knaves inspire you."

The classical and mediaeval aspects of Japan have been obscured by the changes of recent decades, although they have not entirely disappeared. Since the Second World War, the world of business has been pervaded by new influences. Industrial magnates like those of twentieth-century Britain and America, self-made men of immense energy and capacity, and also a great army of assiduous and meticulous executives and bureaucrats, typical of our own day, have come to the fore.

Most Japanese, with experience of life in the West, agree that one of the most marked differences between themselves and Europeans lies in the contrast between our individualism and their preference for acting as part of a group. The contrast has been exaggerated in popular discussion, and I have never been conscious of it when in the society of intimate friends. It is true that when a Japanese is engaged in an important transaction, or when he has to take decisions, he likes to be fortified by the presence of his family, or his professional or business associates, and to act as the spokesman of a group. It is sometimes difficult to persuade a Japanese to give his own opinion on a controversial subject. He may be uneasy if pressed to do so. He generally prefers to talk things over with his associates and then to offer the group opinion. Decisions about careers or marriages were once, and still are to a large extent, taken only after long discussions in family councils.

How Others See Us

A similar practice is customary before arriving at business decisions. The West, in the last decade, has heard much about the Japanese managerial practice of *ringisei*, that is, the system by which proposals oscillate between different grades of staff with the aim of reaching a consensus that can be put to the president of the firm. It is a system that consumes much time in discussion. However, once a decision has been reached, execution is rapid because everyone concerned knows what is involved and is committed to it.

The developments of the last half-century have brought modifications but not fundamental changes in these respects. Because decisions are so often taken by groups (and sometimes by a number of interrelated groups) it is often difficult to detect where power really resides. There are, however, exceptions to this rule. Some of the largest industrial enterprises that have been built up since the War owe their success to the leadership of a few persons with strongly marked individuality. Yet, in general, even founders of great businesses, for all their drive and force, take little pride in domination, and seek rather to blend themselves with the organisations they have called into being. The main aim is, usually, to create in the company a permanent body of institutions and a style of industrial behaviour that will mould the attitudes of those recruited into its service.

This pervasive characteristic of the Japanese – the reluctance of individuals to commit themselves or to take decisions without consultation with their fellows – has been a source of exasperation to foreigners who have had professional or business dealings with them. It leads to delays which foreigners find inexcusable and to obfuscation as the Japanese try to find means for staving off impatient demands for clear-cut decisions. Hence, the Japanese earned a reputation in many quarters of being devious and untrustworthy, a view held by the Jesuit missionaries of the sixteenth century, Saint Francis Xavier and Alessandro Valignano, who otherwise found much to admire in the

Japanese character. Yet this is a complete misunderstanding. In my experience, and in that of most of my friends who have known them well, the Japanese can be relied on to carry out their engagements meticulously although they do not always fulfil their obligations in the way that one expects.

Before leaving this question of mutual misunderstanding, I must refer to a recent episode. In the spring of 1979 I had the honour of a short interview with Prime Minister Ohira. In the course of our conversation, he asked "I believe that Europeans have difficulty in understanding the Japanese, is this so?" When I told him that it was so, he added: "But so do I, so do I." I mentioned this remark to some Japanese friends who were much amused and said: "And we have difficulty in understanding him." Perhaps we must all be content to misunderstand one another with good humour.

I soon found that to live in Japan without nervous strain it was necessary to come to terms with their technique of social intercourse. In effect, this meant that, since the Japanese are generally good-natured and generous, one could often have one's own way in matters of substance provided that one conformed to the conventions. The Japanese are sensitive in personal relationships and are easily offended or hurt by discourtesy, although they show themselves ready to make allowances for social solecisms that do not proceed from carelessness or ill-intention. It is barbarous to refuse invitations bluntly or to return a direct negative to proposals. An inclination to accept or confirm should be suggested by circumlocutions. The hint is quickly taken and no loss of face is incurred. One must be prepared oneself to receive hints or delicately proposed suggestions, and those who are not may find themselves, as they think, let down by what they regard as equivocation. I found that when I was asking for directions or for an opinion, I had to remember that a stranger prefers to return an answer that is likely to please.

The world has always admired the capacity of the Japanese for self-control. It is rare for them to lose their tempers however great the provocation, and they do their utmost to hide their deepest emotions. Sometimes this self-restraint is carried to lengths that may seem shocking to outsiders. An English friend of mine expressed his sympathy with a servant who had just lost a child. "No matter," said the bereaved parent with a smile, "I have three more." This response was not the mark of a callous disposition. It was produced in obedience to the code which prescribes that one must not inflict one's personal sorrows on others.

The conventions that forbade expressions of emotion or even affection sometimes appeared unbearably harsh. For instance, since the family was a powerfully knit group and stood at the foundation of Japanese society, its welfare had precedence over the happiness of the individuals who composed it. It was considered bad form, even ludicrous, for a married couple to show their devotion to one another. A friend of mine who made a love match was reprimanded by his father-in-law (he had been adopted into his wife's family) for being seen too frequently in her company. He even took her about with him on his motor bicycle! The family as a whole was exposed to ridicule by this conduct.

In those days young men and women never went about together unless they were chaperoned. Even then, the younger people were in revolt against these rigid and austere rules. A young Japanese professional man once said to me that home life in his country lacked the spontaneity and joy that he supposed existed in the West. "*Jishin, kaminari, kaji, oyaji*" (earthquakes, thunder, fire and father) is a Japanese saying descriptive of the four chief terrors of life. Yet changes were on the way. In the 1930s, the disregard for convention by the *moga* (modern girl) and *mobo* (modern boy) in dance halls and cafés brought angry reactions from their elders. The discomfiture of the conservative elements in society at the end of the Second World War, together with the example of the American social habits to which the people were exposed during the Occupation, produced a revolution in manners. Today, the relations between husbands and wives in public are no longer constrained and formal. One of my greatest surprises when I paid my first visit to Japan after the Second World War was to see young men and women enjoying each other's company in cafés or strolling down the Ginza hand-in-hand. This conduct would not have been tolerated in the 1920s. As to the saying quoted above, a Japanese family man told me ruefully that while his country still had to cope with earthquake, fire and thunder, the father had long since ceased to be a terror!

In the early post-war period, the reconciliation of the new freedom with the lingering conventions of chaperonage was not achieved without difficulty. The definition of appropriate conduct had to be redrawn. What had previously been settled by an acknowledged rule now became the subject of debate within the family circle.

The influence of the United States on Japanese society deserves comment. Even before the War it was far greater than that exercised by any other nation. I have already mentioned the predominance of Hollywood films at the cinemas, and relations in business, tourism and educational affairs were comparatively close. Conservative Japanese resented what they regarded as corrupting American influences, and a colleague complained to me that Japan was rapidly degenerating into an American colony. Yet a high proportion of the young loved it all. After the War Americans were in virtual control of Japan for six years and were present in large numbers. The elimination of the military cliques, Japan's architects of ruin, left them with little opposition to their proselytising for the American way of life. The reforms – political, economic, constitutional and educational – were far-reaching and, though they were subsequently modified, their effects endured. Above all, the Americans brought freedom from the traditional restraints that had, in the past, inhibited the development of parliamentary government and the exercise of individual energies in economic affairs. At that time many new undertakings were born and entrepreneurship was in the ascendant.

The permanent social influence of the Allied Occupation is more difficult to judge. Although the restraints of convention have been loosened and family life has become freer, it would be an error to suppose that Japanese society is simply a slightly abnormal or eccentric species of modern industrial society as we know it in the West. For individuals the springs of action are rather different, and social relations, though much changed since the War, are still, from a Western point of view, peculiar. Thus, the acceptance of reciprocal obligation has remained intact. A high proportion of marriages are still arranged through go-betweens. The family group, if less cohesive than in the past, still plays a more important role than in Britain or the United States. The family still regards itself as responsible for assuming much of the burden of social welfare, admittedly to a decreasing extent. For instance, a considerable proportion of elderly relatives continue to reside with their children. Japanese traditional social arrangements, as modified by the liberating influences of the Occupation period, may claim to have furnished a basis for the massive achievements of the last thirty years. Japan supplies a telling example of Toynbee's contention that "the influence of the past is most beneficent when the . . . veneration for it is temperate".

Foreigners who understood Japan's social system far more completely than I did were nevertheless often exasperated by the fatalistic acceptance of mishaps and calamities that they found among their acquaintances. Even when the trouble could be ascribed to bungling, a Japanese was likely enough to respond with the murmur of *shikataganai* ("it can't be helped", or "it is written"). This attitude to misfortune and unpleasantness seems inconsistent with the pertinacity and determination to succeed which has long distinguished the Japanese in their business or professional affairs. The apparent inconsistency, however, can easily be resolved. Their practical capacity shows itself especially in group action and co-operative ventures in which every member of an enterprise is assigned a definite role. In such ventures personal preferences or inclinations are subordinated to the claims of the group. It follows that in these circumstances the individual must not seek to assert himself and must dismiss the vicissitudes that affect him personally with a gesture of resignation.

In France and Britain the vast majority of the population is entirely uninterested in foreign ways. I was quickly struck by the contrast between this attitude and the lively concern of the Japanese with the novel and unfamiliar. It was remarkable that a people with such strong traditions and such rigid rules of conduct should so readily turn their minds to consider how others lived and thought. The explanation is to be found not only in the fact that they realised that Japan had to acquire foreign knowledge in order to gain a respected place among the great nations; there was also real intellectual curiosity, a readiness to try everything, an eagerness to give hospitality to foreign institutions and devices. The Japanese were willing to experiment even if at times the innovation might seem to offend their own traditions or their belief in their unique excellence. In the 1890s Prince Ito, struck by the superior physique of Western peoples, had seriously inquired of Herbert Spencer whether it would be expedient to encourage intermarriage between Europeans and Japanese.

Curiosity extends to all manner of detail. When Japanese are abroad, they like to make quite sure that they understand everything they see and hear. Their curiosity sometimes turns in unexpected directions. A senior Japanese diplomat who made a tour of Ireland was left with only one perplexity which he asked me to resolve for him. It was the meaning of the epitaph which Yeats had written for himself and is now inscribed on the stone over his grave in Drumcliff churchyard:

Cast a cold eye
On life, on death.
Horseman, pass by.

They were, and are, the world's outstanding pragmatists. From my early times in Japan I was frequently asked whether I thought that this or that set of doctrines would make a useful contribution to Japan's progress as a nation. In 1936 the Vice-Minister of Foreign Affairs asked me if I thought that Buchmanism (the so-called Oxford Movement) could provide a useful substitute for some of the old religious beliefs that Japan had lost!

This curiosity about novelties in both artifacts and ideas, and their readiness to find accommodation for intrusions into their civilisation, doubtless explain their adaptability to change. A Japanese friend, a Quaker by religion, gave me an example of the willingness of his countrymen to listen to strange doctrines in a period long before Western ideas had become commonplace to educated men. In his family inheritance he found a copy of the first Chinese translation of the Bible. It had belonged to one of his forefathers, who had added the following inscription: "This is the most curious book that I have ever read. I think that my descendants also will find it interesting and I hope that they will always keep it."

Examples of Japan's capacity to absorb the exotic are innumerable, but that provided by the image of Erasmus is one of the oddest. In 1600 a Dutch ship which carried a figurehead of Erasmus was wrecked off the coast. The figurehead was brought ashore and passed into the possession of one of the *Shogun*'s retainers. Then it vanished from sight until 1919, when it was discovered in the Ryoko-in, a Buddhist temple in the village of Haneda in Tokyo Prefecture. Its adventures in the interval were unravelled by several scholars and are recounted in a paper (*The Image of Erasmus*, Transactions of the Asiatic Society of Japan, 1934) written by a friend of mine, J. B. Snellen, a member of the Dutch diplomatic service who was killed by the Germans in the bombing of Rotterdam.

According to his account, the figurehead had passed from the retainer to the temple in which it was ultimately found. Its origins, however, were soon forgotten. At one time it was thought to have come from Korea and to represent the legendary inventor of ship-building. Subsequently, it achieved a place in the pantheon and at different times it was taken for a number of well-known deities, *Ebisu-sama*, the patron of seafarers and fishermen, *Tanuki* the badger god and even a bogeyman to intimidate little children. It was a strange fate for Erasmus, but no stranger than the Vatican's acceptance of the statue in 1926 as that of a saint of the Roman Catholic Church.

The Japanese themselves are often bewildered when they learn how they are viewed through foreign eyes. Unfortunately I have never been able to discover what they thought of the picture of them presented in that entrancing novel *L'Honorable Partie de Campagne* by Thomas Raucat. This book is too light-hearted to be regarded as a satire but too true to life to be dismissed as a caricature. In my opinion the author's insight into certain of Japan's social postures went very deep. He brought out with sure but delicate strokes the comic aspects of the misunderstandings and gaucheries that often attended intercourse between Europeans and Japanese at a time when Japan was finding her feet in the modern world. Yet he also showed himself to be aware of, and sympathetic with, the poetic melancholy, the sense of *mono no aware* – the *lachrimae rerum* – which among many Japanese was so strangely mingled with their practical capacity.

When I read the book, I did not, of course, think that Raucat had provided an objective and balanced view of the country, but I recognised at once as authentic the pictures that he flashed upon his screen. Today the European resident in Japan would, I suspect, dismiss the book as a travesty or burlesque. The changes of the last sixty years have left little of Raucat's world intact. Japan has come to terms with the West and is at ease in the company of other advanced nations. The incidents which the author described, and which in his day bore a recognisable identity with the experiences of most Europeans in Japan, could scarcely occur in the 1980s – at any rate not in the capital city, where the author had placed them.

Curiosity about the unfamiliar and the exotic goes far

towards explaining the ambiguous attitude of the Japanese to the West. They doubted our moral worth and cast a critical eye on our social behaviour. Yet, from the beginning of the modern era they admired, perhaps extravagantly, our practical capacity and our technological ingenuity. Is it to this that one can attribute their willingness to become pupils of the West? From the time I first went among them it seemed to me that the real source of their interest lay in a certain quality which they found irresistible. This quality was the charm of novelty. Now that they have overtaken Europeans and Americans in economic achievement and share with the West all the benefits that modern industry can provide, the modes by which, until recently, they measured their progress have become irrelevant. So it seems that notable changes both in their own attitude to Western peoples and also their policy towards the outside world are imminent.

I can naturally write more confidently of what Europeans thought of Japanese ways than I can of the opinions held by Japanese about Westerners. Yet, even though courteous people refrain from expressing their judgement in the hearing of those whom they are criticising, one cannot spend some years among them without getting an impression of the attitude of ordinary Japanese to the outside world and to the habits of foreigners. Some of their opinions are decidedly unflattering. From early times the ungainly postures of the over-sized Westerners have been a subject for caricaturists who showed the red-haired visitors sprawling on the *tatami*. The voices of foreigners were disagreeably loud and harsh. Japanese returning from visits to Western countries reported that few foreigners took daily baths and paid little attention to personal cleanliness, especially to ritual washing. The presence of chamber pots in bedrooms and the practice of taking breakfast in bed disgusted some of the early visitors to Europe. Of course, they also found things to admire – for instance, the good roads, the solid buildings and, in general, the affluence of Europe and America.

Rooms in Japanese inns, as in the houses, are divided from one another only by *shoji* or *fusuma*, so it is not possible to lock up one's room, and one is always liable to an unexpected intrusion. Japanese, when they first made contact with the practices of Western hotels, remarked on the privacy that guests required in their bedrooms and bathrooms, although oddly enough, it seemed that they were content to eat together in a common dining room. I once read a thesis in English by a Japanese student of hotel management. He made a great point of the fact that the Japanese hotelier who wanted to cater for foreign guests must provide rooms that could be locked; although, as he said, "the key need not be so tight a one" as in Western hotels.

Sometimes the things that impressed the Far-Eastern visitor to Europe were not those which the native would have expected. A Nagoya colleague told me a story that had gone the rounds about a high official of the Ministry of Education who had been sent to Europe to acquaint himself with the educational systems and with other aspects of Western civilisation. On his return a friend asked him what features of the European scene had surprised him most. He replied: "The size of Frenchwomen's hips."

A friend of mine, on his return from England, told me that he had been shocked, on entering a London restaurant for the first time, to see a notice which stated that the management was not responsible for the safety of its clients' hats and coats hung on the stands provided. A Japanese restaurateur, he said, would feel deeply dishonoured if one of his guests suffered a loss in his establishment, and would feel obliged to make amends. I must add that in Japan in the 1920s, the risk of loss through pilferage was negligible.

Occasionally, a Japanese with advanced views who had acquired a naively idealistic or romantic notion of Europe was disappointed at the reality. In the early 1950s a Japanese woman journalist, left-wing in inclination, told me that she could not understand why, in an England that was enjoying full employment and prosperity, there were still prostitutes to be seen in Piccadilly! While she was in England she visited various local branches of the Labour Party, and her experience there also left her disillusioned. When she enquired of the wives of Party workers why they themselves supported Labour, the most common answer was: "Because my husband does." She had expected to find that Englishwomen – who, she thought, had long been emancipated – would have shown more independence of mind.

The Japanese have often been hurt because foreign visitors failed to appreciate what they themselves regarded as merits in their civilisation. The Prince of Wales came to Japan in the early 1920s and at the end of his stay he was asked to choose a Japanese dress. It caused surprise and some offence when his choice fell on a coolie's costume, complete with *happi* coat. However, his hosts were ready to excuse his lack of appreciation of all their country had to offer in beautiful clothes, by reflecting that the coolie costume came nearest to the European style of dress.

The more advanced or liberally-minded Japanese admired many of the social arrangements of Europe and America. They found their own convention that forbade public expressions of emotion or affection irksome. There was, though, by no means unqualified approval of our ways, even in those quarters. For instance, our marriage arrangements and customs seemed strange even to many sophisticated people who thought them unfair to large numbers of women. A young university lecturer who spent some months in a boarding house in London certainly came to that conclusion. He said to me: "In my boarding house there are many young women, some in their late twenties, who would like to get married but have not found a husband. In Japan their mothers would have arranged a marriage for them years ago."

The large numbers of spinsters of marriageable age in Europe surprised the ordinary Japanese who was unaware that, after the Great War, young women greatly outnumbered young men. A Japanese convert once asked a European woman missionary: "You say that you have never been married, but have you never even been sent back?" (She meant: "Have you not even been returned to your family after the trial period between the Shinto ceremony and the legal registration?")

My housekeeper was an unfailing source of information about the popular view of foreign ways, and as in Nagoya foreigners were few and conspicuous, there was much gossip about them. I treasure one delicious example of a misunderstanding. A house in our neighbourhood was occupied by a middle-aged American missionary who had been left a widower with a small girl and baby son. A lady missionary, out of the goodness of her heart, was looking after his household. She was a refined and charming person whose life had been devoted to her calling, and it might have been expected that her relations with the servants would have been easy and friendly. The reverse was true. The reason for the servants' complaints about her was that, although in their view she was merely a concubine, she conducted herself as if she were the *okusan* (wife). My housekeeper obviously thought that this pretence fully justified the servants' disaffection.

British visitors to Japan in Victorian times noticed that Japanese children were allowed liberties denied to their own. They were seldom reproved and this treatment seemed inconsistent with the rigid constraints imposed upon adults. The Japanese, in their turn, when they came to see something of British social life, commented unfavourably on the British way with children. Our ancestors seemed inexcusably harsh towards them.

This was not the only sphere in which the Japanese thought that they had reason to complain of the ill-nature of Westerners. While they regarded themselves as essentially a kindly and considerate people, the popular stereotype of the Westerner was just the opposite. I have already mentioned that any display of bad temper was considered to be very bad form by the Japanese. Since their social relations were conducted on a high level of formal courtesy, they were at sea in dealing with situations in which short-tempered foreigners were involved. These occasions were not infrequent. A well-known story, the theme of a famous song (*Tojin Okichi*), revolves round the problem of international intercourse soon after the opening of the country to the West.

The story illustrates both the embarrassment of the Japanese at displays of bad manners and also their realism in their attempts to find a solution. The officials who had to deal with Townsend Harris, the first United States representative in Japan, were troubled by the frequency with which he lost his temper, the result probably of the equivocations which he had to put up with. They discussed this propensity among themselves and came to the conclusion that it could be attributed to the lack of female company. So they persuaded a *geisha*, Okichi, to take up residence with Harris in the hope that she would be able to soothe his troubled spirit. Poor Okichi was ill-rewarded for her patriotism. Although her self-sacrifice was applauded, she suffered social ostracism and contempt for her association with a Western barbarian. Hence the opprobrious term, *Tojin Okichi* (equivalent to "dago Okichi").

The foreigner was popularly regarded as a creature of uncertain mood. More than this, it was alleged that, in contrast to the kindly Japanese, Westerners were actually cruel. It is only recently that I heard how they are supposed to have acquired this characteristic. Europeans have always been meat-eaters and stock raisers. They bring up their animals carefully and even get to know them as individuals. Then deliberately, and in cold blood, they kill them. This practice, pursued for centuries, has coarsened and hardened their minds. The Japanese, on the other hand, being grain-eaters, have not been exposed to these debasing influences. Buddhist doctrine is no doubt responsible for these views. Even in modern times workers in leather, butchers and others employed in trades offensive to Buddhist doctrine have been found almost entirely among the descendants of the *eta* (outcasts). The *eta* are known officially in modern Japan by a less opprobrious term, *suiheisha* (society of declassed people). The ordinary Japanese still refer to them as *eta*.

It is clear that the ideas of Westerners and Japanese about each other's character and conduct have been strongly influenced by popular myths. It is my belief that most people who have lived for any length of time in Japan have carried with them the impression of a courteous and good-natured people. Even so it may well be true, as a former British ambassador said, that the Japanese are nicer to foreigners than they are to each other. They have blind spots, yet on the whole they are a people of quick sympathies which may have ampler opportunities for expression today than at the time when conventional restraints were more rigid. This view is contrary to the opinion held of the Japanese by the majority of Europeans. Before the Second World War they were regarded as bellicose and aggressive, although these attributes were applied to the nation as a whole rather than to the conduct of individuals in their everyday life, about which the ordinary European knew nothing.

It was the behaviour of the army towards its prisoners which gained for the Japanese a reputation for inhumanity and barbarism. This behaviour the Allies have found hard to forgive. Various explanations have been proffered. It is said that while in past wars the conduct of the Japanese towards their prisoners was correct, standards deteriorated during the 1930s, partly because of the brutalising discipline to which the soldiers were subjected. It is sometimes argued that since it was held to be the duty of a Japanese soldier to die rather than to surrender, any prisoners taken were looked on with contempt. None of this is very convincing.

It is not easy to discuss these matters frankly with Japanese. They are inclined to shy away from the subject as they do from discussions of the atomic bombing of Hiroshima and Nagasaki. Some of them, however, have commented upon the charges levelled against them. Whilst not attempting to deny that cruelties occurred, they argue that these did not proceed from any especially evil qualities in the Japanese character, but from the circumstances of war itself. Atrocities, they rightly say, are committed by all armies in wartime, although they would agree that there is a difference between atrocities committed by ill-disciplined soldiers in the field and those that result from a deliberate act of policy on the part of the High Command. The nature of this reply is symptomatic of the way in which the postwar generation looks upon the past. It holds that it has broken with the country's former policies; it does not admit any identity between itself and the militarists of the 1930s and 1940s, who are now dead or have been thrust into obscurity. I doubt if it is useful to pursue this question any further here.

I shall conclude this chapter of misunderstanding on a lighter note. It is easy for even a careful observer to go astray in his interpretation of the behaviour of foreigners. He is liable to overlook the significant and to base his opinions on what is to him exotic and unfamiliar. Japanese readers of this book will no doubt detect many instances of this error. However, I can recall one case in which a Japanese friend of mine shared with me the fault of jumping to confident conclusions on inadequate evidence.

To the north of Chiba Prefecture there is a region called Itako, sometimes referred to as Japan's Lake District. Here tourists are taken along a network of canals in boats punted by women in old-fashioned country costumes and the wide straw hats once worn by all farmers. The friend who accompanied my wife and myself on an excursion to Itako remembered that a few years previously the boats had been worked by men. We speculated about the reasons for the change, and found no difficulty in deciding that the increasing shortage and rising cost of male labour was responsible. This, we said, was a particular example of the prevailing trend; throughout Japan agricultural workers were moving in large numbers to the cities to take up more highly paid work. To confirm our diagnosis we asked the woman who was punting our boat for an explanation. She replied that the change had occurred because it was found that women dressed in traditional costumes looked more picturesque than men and attracted more tourists. So much for economic analysis!

VI

Manners, Moods and Convictions

In the vestibule of the Faculty Club of a leading Tokyo university there is inscribed on the panelling the injunction that members in using the Club should forget their class order, that is to say, that they should not allow their behaviour to fellow-members to be influenced by seniority in the year of graduation. The notice interests a British guest, for it would never occur to him that there would be any need to give such counsel to members of a similar club in Britain. When I saw this notice a few years ago, my mind turned at once to a characteristic of Japanese social arrangements which had impressed me from my earliest contacts with the country. This is the general acceptance of the principle of hierarchy, a principle which seems to have been transmitted unimpaired from feudal times.

In the 1920s it was more evident than it is now, for the deference paid by inferiors to superiors was attended by ceremonious forms of behaviour which have since been modified. Communications between different ranks or orders accorded with this principle. Inferiors addressed their superiors in polite and elaborate phrases, while superiors used abrupt and curt speech towards inferiors. This convention did not excite resentment. I found that the respect of the students at the *Koto Shogyo Gakko* for their Principal, who was a dignified and distinguished person, was if anything enhanced by the fact that he used the less polite forms of speech in addressing them.

Appointment in Japan

The application of the principle of hierarchy, though it sometimes created tension, bore less harshly on the inferiors than might have been expected. I soon came to understand that it gave rise to a reciprocal obligation. For one party there was the acceptance of rank and unqualified loyalty to a superior; for the other party there was a responsibility, enforced by convention and public opinion, for the welfare of those who served him or were under his tutelage. Even in those days the employer could not discharge workers without providing what we should now call redundancy payments, and as large-scale industry grew up the employer assumed extensive responsibilities for his employees' well-being. The life-long employment system, by which a school-leaver once taken on by a firm can expect to remain in that firm's employment until retirement, was once regarded as an example of paternalism. In the last twenty-five years it has received a wide application throughout industry and accords with the concept of the firm as an association of men of varying grades and functions, but with a common purpose. The effect of the system on the managerial and executive staff is that even today it is rare for a manager to move to a position outside the firm or group in which he has begun his career. When it happens, such a transference is still regarded with some suspicion.

The general acceptance of the hierarchical principle meant, of course, that all members of a group had an assured and defined place in it, and that it was unnecessary for anyone to assert his status, whatever it might be. This had the effect of allowing relations between inferiors and superiors to be relaxed and easy. The master might be exacting in his treatment of his servants, but he was not aloof from them. In the intimacy of the family circle they joined easily in conversation and jokes.

In foreign households with Japanese servants differences in etiquette and master–servant relations sometimes led to surprises. These were most likely to occur if the mistress of the foreign household tried to run her establishment as she would have done at home. I once attended a formal dinner party given by a foreign resident at which one of the maids, an elderly woman, was obviously the victim of a scarcely restrained urge to make her own comments on the progress of the meal. Her chance came at the end of the party. The conversation had hitherto been conducted in English, but the chief guest – an American – as he rose from his seat, thanked his host and hostess in a conventional Japanese phrase. The maid, hearing at last some words in her own language, assumed that they were addressed to her and replied genially to the astonished guest, in a phrase that can be translated: "Sir, we shall be friends for life."

This relationship extended to industrial life also. Once when I was going over a large factory, the manager, who had had business experience in Europe, pointed out with pride that all members of the executive staff, including himself, normally had their lunch with their workpeople in the firm's canteen. He had observed that in large British firms there is a descending order of lunch rooms to which employees are assigned, according to their status in the firm. In the middle 1950s, when I went to see one of the great modern steel works, I noted that the manager contented himself with a small austere office and with clothing that was indistinguishable from that of his workers.

The hierarchical system required that everyone's status should be unambiguously clear. Until a Japanese has placed a new acquaintance in an appropriate niche, he is uneasy and reserved. Once he has done so, the barriers are thrown down. I found that, in my own researches into the Japanese economy, hesitations on the part of those to whom I went for information disappeared as soon as they were clear about my status. In 1936 I spent some time in Japan in order to research into Japan's industrial development. The project had been initiated and organised by Harvard University and Radcliffe College. Those to whom I went for information thought it strange that a professor from a British University should be engaged on a specifically American research project. They were reassured when they learned that I had formerly taught at a Japanese college and had specialised in industrial economics.

Politically, 1936 was a year of tension and Japan was suspicious of foreign investigators. In the course of my visit I stayed for a short time with a Canadian family. After I had left, the police pestered my hosts with enquiries about me. It seemed very suspicious that they had given hospitality to one who was a stranger to them, but they were reassured when they learned that I had been introduced by one of my host's English relatives who was a neighbour of mine at home.

This example brings out the importance of the go-between in Japanese business and social life. To him is allotted the responsibility of introducing and guaranteeing the standing of a newcomer to any circle so that a relationship of confidence can be established. In the arrangement of marriages he was (and still is) called upon by a family in search of a spouse for a son or a daughter. His function is to effect the introductions and to smooth the path to suitable alliances. In social as in business affairs, the use of an intermediary avoids the embarrassment that might attend a direct confrontation between the interested parties, and makes withdrawal from a provisional commitment easier than would otherwise have been possible. As a foreign resident in Japan I usually found it expedient to conduct such business or social negotiations as were necessary through a helpful colleague or student. My experience led me to the conclusion that, although this method sometimes caused delays in coming to the point, on the whole the institution of the go-between was sensible and civilised.

The fact that everyone had his recognised niche in Japanese society affected a wide range of activities and was the basis of some interesting trading conventions which survived in my day. For instance, small village shopkeepers would sometimes charge a higher price per unit if one bought three or four units than if one bought a single one. This practice, it was explained to me, was justified on the grounds that a customer who asked for several units was clearly well-off and could thus afford to pay a higher price than the poor fellow who had to be content with one. The practice is not so irrational as it seems. Indeed, the economist might say that this is a method by which the shopkeeper transfers the consumer surplus, which normally accrues to the purchaser, to himself. But obviously it could only work satisfactorily in a society governed by certain social conventions. Thus, one is prompted to ask why the well-to-do purchaser should not defeat the shopkeeper's efforts to charge him a higher price by making several separate unit purchases. The answer is that in a hierarchical society in which everyone knows the income and standing of others, every purchaser is easily identified and it would be bad form for the well-to-do man to try to evade his obligations. I do not suppose that this convention survives today but I met with several instances of it during the 1920s.

Another convention, which had once been widespread, still survived in remote country places. The arrangement was that the guest at an inn should be charged only prime cost by the landlord. To this charge he was supposed to add a present for service and a payment towards overheads which varied according to his ability to pay. In the old days, when everyone's standing was known, there was little possibility of avoiding one's obligations in this respect. Attempts to do so would have courted the disfavour of a rigidly conventional community. In the circumstances of Japanese life today, as in individualistic societies, it would not be practicable to leave the guest to make his own decision.

The sense of reciprocal obligation which pervades society is expressed in many ways. No doubt the widespread habit of present-giving has its origins in a wish to create an obligation towards the giver on the part of the recipient. It often survives in a vestigial form. I remarked that a packet of stamped postcards was a common token. People who had just taken up residence in our village presented their neighbours with a gift of this kind when they paid their first call. More incongruously, or so it seemed to me, on an occasion when I attended a Buddhist funeral service as one of the mourners, after the ceremony the bereaved relatives handed out stamped postcards to all who had been there.

Even if the Japanese resent the obligations which they may have incurred unwillingly, they are bound to acknowledge them by their conduct. I once had a long discussion with a young Japanese businessman who opened his heart to me on the burdens that *giri* (obligation, duty) imposed; yet there was no question of his ignoring them. Regarded from the standpoint of the nation, *giri* helps to provide the discipline which explains much of its cohesion and strength. Sometimes it is displayed in circumstances of nobility and generosity. It inhabits the world of business and politics as well as the milder regions of social relationships, or those between students and teachers to which I have already referred.

One example of it made a deep impression on an English businessman of my acquaintance. During the 1930s, at the time of the troubles with China, Japanese firms were forced by the hostility of the local government and population to withdraw from the south of the country. The *banto* (executive) of one of the *zaibatsu* (business groups) approached a British merchant firm with offices in the South China ports and asked for such help as the firm could give in protecting the *zaibatsu* interests and property during its absence from the scene. The British firm agreed to do what it could, although in practice it turned out that it was not able to do very much. Just before the outbreak of the Pacific War the British firm asked the same *banto* whether, in the event of war and subject to the latter's obligations to his own government, he would do what he could to safeguard its properties, if these should have to be abandoned. Without hesitation, the *banto*, mindful of his past obligations, consented, and in the event the British firm had cause to be grateful for the protection actually afforded.

Sir George Sansom has given another example. Just before the Second World War he had been associated with a group of Tokyo literary men in providing a memorial for an ancient Japanese poet, but the War broke out before the stone had been cut. When he visited Japan a few months after fighting had ceased, he was touched to find that the stone was in position and that his name (though that of an enemy) had been included in the list of celebrants. Thus, the Japanese sense of honour and obligation was not entirely submerged even during the darkest days of aggressive nationalism.

Ritual and ceremony played an essential part in life. Whenever acquaintances met they exchanged prolonged greetings, bowing low to each other as they murmured the conventional phrases. Business negotiations were always preceded by the drinking of tea, a ceremony which was often protracted. If one paid a social call, tea and rice cakes were provided, and I was surprised to find that if I did not consume my portion it was handed over to me in a little package by the maid when I left. It was obligatory to give presents on certain occasions, and when these took a traditional form they often surprised Western recipients. On my departure from Japan several friends who had come to see me off at Nagoya station handed me gifts which consisted of a length of narrow cotton cloth and some dried bonito, fish which looked and felt like small boomerangs. In the old times, fish was the most usual present. When some other article was substituted for it, the fish was represented by a symbolic paper figure tied to the wrapping. This practice still survives. Sometimes the boxes and containers for the presents were themselves of beautiful construction.

At New Year, the great festival of Japan, convention required that the head of the family should leave cards for all friends and acquaintances. He might find himself spending much of the holiday in making the round of his neighbours in a rickshaw. Wherever he made a call, he was liable to be regaled with *sake*. At New Year it was obligatory for inferiors to take notice of their superiors. For instance, it would have been churlish in the extreme if any member of a teaching staff failed to send greetings to his Principal. The obligation ran through the whole of the community. On New Year's Day, 1923, in bitter weather, I stood outside the moat of the Imperial Palace in Tokyo, near the Twin Bridges, and watched the notables on their way to give their greetings to the Emperor. The military and naval officers were in full dress uniforms and the civilians in frock-coats. Most of them arrived in rickshaws, a few in horse-drawn carriages.

I have referred already to the various domestic ceremonies and the rituals of the home. The services of Shinto priests were called upon to bless the site when a new house was about to be built, and at many factories it was thought proper to install a Shinto shrine. When I complimented a manager on the fine new shrine which had just been placed in the factory compound, he said, with a twinkle: "Yes, business has picked up quite a lot since we built that."

The Mikimoto firm, the famous producers of cultured pearls, used to hold annual memorial ceremonies before a shrine for the spirits of the oysters killed in the course of the trade. I heard also of a ceremony at a clothing factory where the factory-girls commemorated the spirits of the needles broken during the previous year. Those who had received a modern education did not take literally, even at that time, the religious beliefs in which these practices were rooted, but the ritualistic observances themselves were regarded as appropriate and seemly. They were a token, perhaps, of an acceptance, usually vague and ill-defined, of responsibility for the consequences of actions on the part of those who initiated them, a reverence for the life of the world, even for inanimate things.

Adherents of Buddhism and Christianity found nothing inconsistent in these Shinto rituals. Buddhism has never been an exclusive religion, and even the jealous God of the Christians has not succeeded in ousting the shrines from the affections of Japanese converts. There are Christian mothers who never fail to announce the birth of their children to the spirits of the hearth and home. If it seems strange that a modern Japanese should still conform to these traditions, one should remember that in a Japanese family group everyone is likely to defer to the beliefs or prejudices of the senior and more conservative members.

The most solemn rituals were those connected with the Imperial House. I took part annually in a ceremony of a kind that was held in every educational establishment in the country on the Emperor's birthday. The whole College was assembled, the students in their best uniforms, the staff in frock-coats (with carpet slippers or mules) and the Principal in court dress. The Emperor's photograph, which had been kept in a fire-proof strongroom, was placed on a dais and slowly unveiled. The company bowed low, the Imperial Rescript on Education, affirming patriotism and loyalty to the Emperor, was read by the Principal and the National Anthem was sung. The photograph had to be guarded night and day. If it were lost, the head of the establishment would have to resign.

On these occasions everyone showed the deepest reverence but there were, no doubt, private reservations. On one occasion when a schoolmaster friend of mine refused an invitation to dine because it was his turn to guard the photograph at his school throughout the night, I commiserated with him. He replied sententiously: "But it is my privilege" and winked. I doubt if his attitude was typical. The vast majority of the Japanese saw no reason to question the truth of the myths that clustered round the Emperor. They took no objection to the rule that when the Emperor passed through the streets no one should look down on his carriage from an upper storey. He had to be shielded against the unclean and sordid. In applying this principle, the Court officials neglected no detail. The horses which drew the Emperor's carriage had little baskets attached to their hind quarters so that he might be spared the indignity of having to pass over their droppings.

The liking for ritual and ceremony went very deep. It was not only demonstrated on formal occasions and in public affairs but also expressed spontaneously in chance encounters. A European colleague of mine used to walk every day to the College along paths among the paddy fields and *daikon* fields. One day he met a group of three small schoolgirls in their ugly blue uniforms. The smallest of them, who was carrying a large paper umbrella, stopped, bowed, and pointing to my colleague's hat, said: "*chiisana boshi*" (a little hat). With much presence of mind and an admirable sense of occasion he replied: "*okina kasa*" (a large umbrella). The child bowed again and they went their ways. For some months afterwards, whenever the parties met one another, the ritual was repeated. Solemnly and without any simper of embarrassment by herself or her friends, the umbrella-bearing child stopped as my colleague approached, bowed and said: "*chiisana boshi*". He in his turn raised his hat, returned the bow and replied: "*okina kasa*". No other word was ever uttered.

I found that sometimes the Japanese tried to personalise the spirit or corporate character of an enterprise. For example, the Fukusuke Tabi Company, which was at one time a large-scale producer of Japanese-style socks but with the change of fashion turned to many other products, has taken as its symbol a quaint figure of a squatting boy with large-lobed ears. This also appears as its trade mark. It was explained to me that the form of this figure had been modified over the years to accord with the changes in the firm's own personality, and in the structure of its business.

I took a keen interest in Japan's numerous superstitions. I was warned against sleeping with my head to the north, as that was the direction in which corpses were laid. I disregarded this warning to the dismay of my housekeeper! Not long ago I found that a former student of mine had changed his first name. I did not have the opportunity to ask him the reason and I went to someone else for an explanation. I was told that the change was to be explained either because one of the characters in which the name was written had been abolished by the post-war linguistic reforms, which were undertaken to simplify the language, or that my ex-student had been told by a soothsayer that the character was unlucky.

Manners, Moods and Convictions

I was interested to find that the fox is supposed to possess magical powers and that there were many stories about the spells he casts. The uncle of a colleague of mine was quite convinced that he had been charmed by a fox in his young days. His story ran like this. One evening when he was returning from a party a fox ran across his path. He neglected to take the precaution of protecting himself against enchantment by wetting his forefinger with saliva and rubbing it along his right eyebrow. Presently, as he went on his way, he met a beautiful and apparently compliant girl. He put his arm around her and caressed her. Then he lost consciousness, and in the cold light of dawn he awoke to find his arm around a tree and the palm of his hand chafed by friction on the rough bark.

My housekeeper treated with respect all the superstitions which she recounted to me, even if she had reservations about some of them. She believed that the animals wept on the anniversary of *Gautama*'s death, and she told me of the remarkable case of the local eel fisher whose child suffered from an eye disease. Whenever the fisherman made a good catch the disease became worse. When this connection had been definitely established, the fisherman had to give up his trade. Those who suppose that these stories and superstitions, which are derived from Buddhist doctrine, would make the Japanese particularly kind to animals, forget that it is foolish to expect consistency in human conduct. Some superstitions have a practical justification. For instance, during a violent thunderstorm I found my housekeeper crouching low on the *tatami* with her wooden *geta* on her head. She explained to me that the attentions of the god of lightning would be deflected in disgust from such lowly objects. She had at least a qualified belief in the effectiveness of prayers and offerings to the various shrines, including the shrine to the kitchen god. I have already mentioned that she was confident that her daughter's illness had been cured by a visit to the habitation of the local deity with special curative powers.

I liked to think that the shrines, especially those haunted

by the spirit of rocks, rivers and waterfalls, linked the natural world with that of man and helped to strengthen the aestheticism that has had such a prominent place in Japanese civilisation. However, among the mass of the people, belief in these deities went along with a certain earthy cynicism about the claims of religious doctrine. I once asked my housekeeper to explain the significance of the attitude of a certain statue of Buddha which had one hand stretched forward with the palm upward and the other raised with thumb and forefinger describing a circle. I had supposed that it might be an invitation to the worshipper to offer his soul to the universal being and so to escape from the unending circle of life and death. My housekeeper's interpretation was of quite a different order. "It means," she said, "*Ozeni wo kudasai*" (Money, please). It was clear that she was more conscious of the exactions of the begging priest than of philosophic doctrine. She was evidently not alone, for there is a Japanese proverb "*Amida no hikari, mo kane shidai*", which has been translated as "No penny, no paternoster."

The general attitude towards money, as towards several other concomitants of modern civilisation, still reflected past conditions. In the old order the *Samurai* were supposed to hold money and money-getting in contempt. I found that the making or receiving of certain payments was an operation that called for some delicacy. We always handed over our housekeeper's wages in a sealed envelope, and this practice applied to some other payments.

Japan was then, and has remained, one of the few countries where tipping is not expected. In modern hotels, a percentage charge for service is included in the bill, but beyond this tips are not given and are, indeed, refused if offered. Taxi drivers expect to be paid the exact fare. On one occasion a taxi driver mistook his way and so lengthened the journey to my destination. When I gave him the fare indicated on the meter, he gave me some of it back. The absence of tipping adds greatly to the dignity and pleasure of everyday relationships.

Manners, Moods and Convictions

Although the foreigner in Japan soon comes to recognise the extent to which behaviour is governed by rigid convention, he cannot easily discover whether there are many individuals who resent this pressure. Since the Japanese are so practised in self-restraint it is seldom that an outsider is given a glimpse of their feelings in these matters. Occasionally, in my experience, the resentment came to the surface, but this was always among people who had had some acquaintance with the freer social life of the Western world. For a minority of such people, especially if they were of a wayward disposition, life might be miserable. For centuries Western Europeans who have found conditions in their own countries intolerable have been able to try their luck in other lands, whereas for the Japanese there were few opportunities for emigration. In feudal times the pressure had been even stronger and then suicide was the only way of escape from onerous obligations or of protest against intolerable claims.

The social pressures were modified as Japanese society came under Western influences, but during the inter-war period they were still strong and suicide remained a socially approved form of protest. I observed that the newspapers frequently gave prominence to stories of the tragic outcome of the conflict between social responsibility and personal self-expression. Love affairs which ran counter to duty to the family often led to double suicides. Yet even the means chosen for these desperate acts were affected by convention or fashion. At one time, it was the Kegon waterfall, at another time, the railway tracks, and at yet other times, the cliffs, or an outlying island, or a volcano.

The conflicts which gave rise to these tragedies were discussed at length between the supporters of convention and those sympathetic to the rebels. One example of this type of discussion impressed me because of the nature of the arguments put forward on each side. At the time of my first residence in Japan, one of the *genro* had taken a *geisha* of whom he was fond into his household. Presently the *geisha* fled with a young lover and left the old man disconsolate.

The episode was widely reported and debated in the newspapers. The contestants fell into two camps. There were those who held that the *geisha*'s patriotic duty was to remain with the great *genro*, one of the makers of modern Japan, and to comfort him in his old age. The modernists argued, on the other hand, that she was right in answering the call of youthful love.

This case did not end tragically, and it must be said that with the exercise of ingenuity some conventions could be circumscribed. In other words, the social obligations which were real and compelling would have been intolerable if they could not at times have been evaded. Let me give an example.

I once went to stay with my friend of university days in a country district in Central Japan. He was anxious to show me all the sights of his neighbourhood, and he drew up a programme of visits which required a good deal of travelling. At that time the government was worried about the balance of payments and was urging people to curb their expenditure. My friend was a considerable landowner and also had substantial industrial interests in the nearby town. He was, therefore, expected to set a good example. Duty to his guest was in conflict with his patriotic duty. He thought that to hire a car for our expeditions would be regarded as extravagant and would invite criticism, for in those days a car was a great luxury. At the same time he had to meet the claims of hospitality and the weather was hot and the distances considerable. He solved the problem by taking me by train to a point well outside the district where he was well-known, and there he hired a car.

The strain imposed by the unremitting devotion to duty has always had to be relieved if reasonable serenity of mind was to be maintained. In the past this relief was found in aesthetic pursuits or by a temporary withdrawal into the world of natural beauty. Aestheticism is still actively cultivated, although in present-day Japan it sometimes seems to be fighting a losing battle. Many employers, however, have tried to maintain this tradition by making provision for their female workers to be instructed in flower arrangement and the tea ceremony. Some industrial firms, conscious of the strain of modern business life on their executives, occasionally send them to *zen* monasteries for periods of spiritual refreshment.

I have been constantly surprised by the complete change of mood which a Japanese undergoes when he leaves his public and professional activities and returns to the private world of the family and his own nature. Hard, competitive and extrovert in his former capacity, he is contemplative and withdrawn in the second. He seems to inhabit two distinct worlds.

In Japan, or so it seemed to me, the arts give expression mainly to the private voice. They occupy quiet havens beyond ambition and conflict, a retreat from the world of action. I am encouraged in this opinion by learning that when, during the Second World War, the government commissioned the preparation of a collection of patriotic poems by a hundred poets, the scholars entrusted with the task reported that it was not possible to find so many. While the Japanese are an intensely patriotic people and have long been convinced of their high national destiny, it is not in patriotism that the poet has sought inspiration. The beauty of nature, the transitoriness of life, private emotions, aesthetic perception and accomplishment – these are the common themes and preoccupations of the cultivated mind when it is no longer engaged in the practical problems of life.

This proposition must not, of course, be emphasised too strongly. The traditional themes of the Kabuki theatre are concerned with the world of action, the heroes of the civil wars and the sacrifices of individuals in a public or feudal cause. Many of the woodcuts, a form of art once despised by the artistic elite, depicted the "floating world" and workaday life.

The restraint enjoined by the Japanese code of conduct hides from the casual observer the deeply emotional nature of the people. They are quick to respond to sympathy and

Appointment in Japan

understanding; the right word in season may release a flood of emotion. A Japanese acquaintance, a few years after the Second World War, told me of how the hearts of his countrymen were touched by a few sentences spoken by Edmund Blunden. Mr Blunden had pre-war connections with Japan and had once held the Lafcadio Hearn Chair of English Literature at the Imperial University of Tokyo. Just after the end of the War he returned to Japan to lecture. At that time the country lay in ruins. Cities had been destroyed and the people were short of food, clothing and all the necessaries of life. Some were in despair. Others rejoiced to see the end of militarism and welcomed the arrival of what they hoped would be a new era of peace and freedom. For women especially there was the promise of a more fulfilled life. A father would no longer be able to refer to his daughters as *"kane kui mushi"* (money-eating insects)! They had become persons in their own right, and those who so wished had reason to hope that new careers would be open to them.

The perceptive eye of the poet detected the new hopes that were stirring in the midst of the material squalor. In the course of his visit, Mr Blunden was called upon to lecture to a group of young women in an institution with which he had had contacts in his pre-war days. My friend, with tears in his eyes, gave me his version of the poet's opening words: "When I last addressed an audience in this institution, the young women were dressed in fine and elegant clothes. They were all well-groomed, demure and prosperous. Today, everything is changed, your dress is old and shabby, your hair is dull, *but your eyes are shining.*"

It is not easy for a tourist in present-day Tokyo or Osaka to believe in the existence of what George Sansom called the "Japanese genius for the Exquisite". Nowadays it has to seek expression in nooks and crannies away from the main current of national life. While good taste and an appreciation of the beauty of the natural world survive among members of the older generation, I sometimes fear that many of the young have repudiated them. In my day these qualities were taken for granted. They were expressed in domestic architecture, in the simplest objects of everyday use, and in the most popular enjoyments. It is true that excursions to see the cherry blossoms in spring or for moon-viewing, or to see the maples in autumn, were often simply occasions for social relaxation and drinking, yet the pleasure that most Japanese found in the beauty of the scene was real enough.

An example of the ready response of the people to natural beauty came to my notice early in my Japanese career. An American friend had taken a picture to be framed and went to collect it on the day it was to be ready. The picture-framer regretted that the work had not been finished and offered as a reason the fact that there had been a snowfall. My friend did not see the relevance of that event until it was explained to him that the men in the workshop had naturally been distracted from their tasks by the beauty of the snow-clad scene. The explanation may easily have been an excuse for slackness, but the fact that it was offered as a plausible reason for the delay is itself a symptom of the existence of aesthetic feeling widely distributed among the people in those days.

Nevertheless, it was evident then that Japanese taste was in danger of corruption. It was secure when it was concerned with the traditional, but the young were interested mainly in the new artistic horizons that contact with the West had revealed to them. Traditional artistic feeling was of no help to them when they attempted to follow Western models, and some atrocities resulted. This, of course, was a temporary phase and even then some Japanese found themselves at home in both worlds. Their catholicity was demonstrated in a concert given by the Imperial Musicians which I attended in 1924. The first half of the programme consisted of works of Western classical music. The musicians came before us in full evening dress. After the interval they reappeared in ancient court costumes and proceeded to play traditional music on instruments never seen on Western concert platforms.

The performance was in some ways characteristic of the dual life of the educated class at that time, a life which could be inferred from the kinds of goods and services they used. In their amusements, diet and house furnishings there were two recognisably distinct styles. At that period and for many years afterwards the Western and the native forces in Japanese life ran in separate channels. This duality added substantially to the cost of living; for instance, a middle-class Japanese had to possess two distinct sets of clothing. It may also explain some of the inconsistencies of personal conduct and of national policy.

Today, it seems to me that to a large extent the two have coalesced into a unique quality, neither Western nor Eastern as these terms are commonly understood. The assurance with which Japan now handles her affairs may be attributable in part to this successful fusion. She had a similar experience in the past, when she absorbed, and in some measure transformed, the institutions and artistic forms imported from China. At the present time many of the importations from the West are no longer identified as such; they have become part of the Japanese substance. This applies, for example, to food. In the 1920s there was a clear-cut distinction between foreign and Japanese meals, and the former were regarded as strange and exotic. Nowadays they are both varieties of the Japanese cuisine. A similar process of absorption has happened before. *Sukiyaki*, which is now regarded by most foreigners as a typical Japanese dish, was originally an innovation to the diet introduced as the result of contacts with the Dutch. The Japanese word for bread, *pan*, came in through the Portuguese and cannot be written in any character; but bread is not now regarded as a foreign-style food.

The formality of manners, and the anxiety of the Japanese to be on their best behaviour when they are abroad, conceal from foreigners who have only a superficial acquaintance with them, their liking for fun and their keen sense of humour. I shall have more to say about these qualities when I come to write about experience at parties

Manners, Moods and Convictions

which afford ample scope for gaiety, etc. Here, two examples of the sort of things that amuse them may be in place. The cultivated Japanese have an appreciation of irony, and a friend once went out of his way to ensure that I should share his pleasure in a delightful incongruity. During the Occupation, the Americans removed most of the statues of Japanese military and naval leaders. They did not disturb Saigo Takamori, the famous leader of the Satsuma rebellion of 1876, on the ground that he was a political hero rather than a military man. However, the Americans insisted on removing the statue of General Terauchi, usually regarded as an arch-militarist. In his place they set up a symbolic group of nymphs, a form of art unknown to Japanese tradition. The (former) Viscount Kato, a friend of the West and an opponent of the military, took me to see this replacement. He found much amusement in reflecting on the wrath of Terauchi in Valhalla on learning that his statue had been replaced by that of three naked women.

It did not take me long to discover the Japanese delight in puns. Their language, with its numerous homonyms, affords them unrivalled opportunities for this kind of wit, and those of my colleagues who knew English well used to try to extend their practice of it into the foreign field. Two examples of punning remain in my mind. The first refers to an occasion when an Englishman made capital out of this propensity.

I have already referred to the presence of one of the Mitsui family among the early students in W. J. Ashley's Faculty of Commerce at the University of Birmingham. The Japanese never forget their obligations to their teachers. Accordingly, in the early 1920s, when the House of Mitsui sent a delegation of high officials to Europe, it included Birmingham in its tour and did not forget the University. A dinner was held attended by W. J. (then Sir William) Ashley and the delegation, and the question of an endowment to the Faculty of Commerce was raised. The delegation was led by Mitsui's chief *banto*, Baron Takuma Dan, and when the time approached for Ashley to make an after-dinner speech, he asked his neighbour if the name *Dan* had any special significance. He was told that the word had many meanings. *Dan* (or *Danshaku*) meant Baron; it also meant decision, and step. *Dan-dan* could be translated as gradually. With all these opportunities presented to him, Ashley had no difficulty in introducing into his speech an amusing and meaningful play on the word. His punning delighted his hearers and he always believed that it clinched the decision to give the endowment for what became the Mitsui Chair of Finance at the University of Birmingham.

The other example also concerns Takuma Dan and to my mind the pun on this occasion was in the worst of taste. In 1931, when a group of young officers were attacking parliamentary government and the great business houses which were held to be responsible for Japan's troubles, a fanatic murdered Baron Dan on the steps of one of Mitsui's Tokyo offices. Some Japanese ghoulishly murmured to one another "*dan dan dan dan*" literally, "Baron Dan, on the steps, gradually".

I suppose that most foreigners soon became aware of a paradox, the coexistence of fragility with an essential toughness. Thus, some of the most beautiful artifacts were of flimsy construction, and many of the most famous buildings were made of materials vulnerable to fire, storm and earthquake. The result was, even in my time, that the really ancient structures in Japan were much fewer than might have been expected in a country with such a long history. I remember my surprise on learning that the lovely house which belonged to the father-in-law of a friend, a house which looked as if it had been settled for centuries in the tranquil garden that enclosed it, had only recently been uprooted from Tokyo and re-erected in Nagoya. The present-day tourist is not usually aware that the Kinkaku-ji, one of the most famous treasures of Kyoto, is a replacement of a building that was burnt down only thirty years ago. What happens is that when famous buildings are destroyed (and this has often happened), they are replaced in exact detail.

George Allen photographed on a visit to Nagoya in 1979

Welcome party for Dr G. C. Allen, attended by members of Nagoya alumni association and the faculty of the Nagoya University School of Economics, March 28 1979, at Nagoya Castle Hotel, Nagoya
from left to right: Mr Kenichiro Ishii (President of the Alumni Association), Mr Katsuhiko Watanabe, George Allen, Mr Yoshishige Taya, Mr Shozo Eguchi, Mr Masatomo Takeshige

Welcome party for Dr G. C. Allen, attended by Tokyo members of the Nagoya alumni association, March 27 1979, at Hotel Okura, Tokyo *from left to right*: Mr Hideo Shimojo, Mr Shigeo Takayama, Mr Isamu Takashima, George Allen, Mr Katsuhiko Ohishi

The Japan Foundation Award Ceremony, 1980
back row: Mr T. Sawada (former Director, Japan Foundation), Mrs Ogawa, Mrs Iwamura, Mr K. Date (Director, Japan Foundation), Professor K. Hayashi (President, Japan Foundation), Mrs Kohn, Mr A. Borton (son of Professor H. Borton), Mr H. Murata (former Director, Japan Foundation), Mr M. Takita (former Director, Japan Foundation)
front row: Mr Y. Ogawa (the Society for the Teaching of Japanese as a Foreign Language), Dr S. Iwamura (Professor Emeritus, Kyoto University), Professor Allen, Mr H. Kohn (former President, Japan Foundation), Professor H. Borton (former President, Haverford College), Mr K. Okano (Africa Society of Japan)

Just as traditional artistic forms have been constantly re-embodied in the course of Japanese history for the delight of the modern observer, so old institutions and practices are sometimes enlisted in the service of the present generation. I have referred to the retreat by hard-pressed businessmen to the *zen* monasteries. A few years ago, to take another example, I visited Omiyakoen, the centre of *bonsai*. In this neighbourhood there are several plantations of dwarf trees with their life histories of many centuries fully recorded. Nearby there are other areas where amateurs cultivate the trees. One of them told me that this activity had been prescribed by his doctor as a cure for high blood pressure. Since some of these trees take several centuries to mature, a man whose ambition it is to avoid the stresses of urgency could hardly have found a more suitable hobby.

VII

Disaster and Discord

By the summer of 1923 I was feeling very much at home in Japan and nothing had occurred to qualify my enjoyment in the succession of new experiences. This euphoria was suddenly dispelled by the Great Earthquake of 1 September 1923. I had, of course, long been aware that Japan was in an earthquake zone. Shipboard acquaintances on the way out had told me that serious disasters of this nature seemed to recur every twenty-five or thirty years. The last one, which had devastated the Osaka area, took place in the middle 1890s. So another was just about due! I heard this prediction with equanimity and scepticism. I even looked forward to experiencing the first shock.

During my first year small tremors were not infrequent. When they happened, the foundationless house with its heavy roof swayed with a different kind of oscillation from that produced by high winds. The timbers creaked; plaster trickled from the walls; and the electric lamps suspended from the ceiling swung to and fro. These disturbances were too small and too brief to cause me alarm, although I was quick to observe that no Japanese ever treated them lightly. For them most of life's troubles might be a subject for jest, but not earthquakes. Personal disasters were hidden in smiles, but on the mention of *jishin* (earthquake) and still more on its actual occurrence, faces took on a sombre expression.

In August 1923 I spent some time in the North of Japan. Towards the end of that month I went to stay for a week at the famous Fujiya Hotel at Miyanoshita in Hakone, a wild and beautiful mountain district not far from Tokyo. From this district one could often get superb views of Mount Fuji floating above the clouds. It was during the summer that I was visited by the only presentiment that has ever come to me, an uneasy feeling that I was likely to be involved in some general or cosmic disaster. As this feeling persisted my mind turned towards a railway accident, for I knew that I was to do a good deal of travelling. Self-deception is easy, and it may be that what followed is simply a coincidence yet I am quite sure in my own mind that this is a faithful record of my feelings and anticipations at that time.

When I arrived at the hotel I found that it was in some confusion. A burglar had just been discovered on the premises. The rest of my stay, however, was tranquil and agreeable. I walked over the mountains to Lake Ashi and looked with interest at *Owaku Dani* (Big Hell), where clouds of sulphurous fumes rise out of the ground. Nowadays this area is traversed by motor roads, but at that time there were only small tracks and mountain paths. The holiday was very enjoyable and the hotel comfortable, indeed, luxurious. Yet, I suddenly decided to cut short my stay and I returned to Nagoya the day before I had intended. My servant who met me at the station was surprised at my unexpectedly early return. Having arrived home safely, I thought that I could dismiss my summer's premonition as nonsense.

The next day, Saturday, 1 September, about noon, while I was writing a letter in my study, the house began to rock. I waited for the oscillations to die away as had always happened on previous occasions, but the swaying of the electric lamps persisted and the whole house seemed to be in motion. From the kitchen and from neighbours' houses there came cries of *"jishin"*. After what seemed to me to be several minutes the oscillations gradually moderated and presently ceased. My housekeeper rushed into my room to ask reproachfully why I had remained in the house. The only safe place in an earthquake, she said, was in the open, well away from the buildings.

Appointment in Japan

I laughed the matter off, restored fallen books to my bookcase and threw away some broken glassware. However, I had hardly resumed writing my letter before the tremors began again. As they were repeated at short intervals throughout the day, it took me some time to finish the letter. Oddly enough it has survived, and I can see from the breaks in it the number of times that I was interrupted. My friend who ultimately received it was astonished to observe that it was written in red ink, and subsequently teased me about it. This, however, must not be taken as further evidence of prescience; I had simply run out of black ink.

By the evening news began to filter through of a terrible disaster in the whole of the Kanto region, including Tokyo and Yokohama. The railways and the telegraph and telephone services ceased to function and we were left, like the rest of the world, at the mercy of rumour. I went frequently to the city centre to read the bulletins posted outside the offices of the local newspaper. These, and the garbled stories of people who had managed to escape from Tokyo, were for some days the only sources of information. I was reminded of the first months of the 1914–18 War when, as a boy, I used to cycle to the headquarters of the local newspaper to read the bulletins posted outside.

Monstrous stories were soon in circulation. Besides the damage caused by the shocks themselves and the huge fires which followed them, a tidal wave (it was said) had engulfed part of the Kanto region. The Korean labourers, who were employed on navvying work, were alleged to have taken advantage of the chaos and to have poisoned the wells. In consequence of these absurd charges, several unfortunates among them were attacked and killed by panic-stricken mobs. The tensions closely resembled those of wartime.

Gradually more authoritative news came to us. People who had made their way over broken roads and damaged bridges at length told us the facts, or some of them. Tokyo and Yokohama had been laid waste by fire and other towns

Disaster and Discord

in the Kanto area had been badly damaged. I found that the hotel at which I had taken lunch at Lake Ashi had collapsed into the water. Thousands had died. Tokyo was full of homeless people in search of lost relatives, and refugees were pouring into the countryside. Nearly 100,000 people died in the earthquake. Half of Tokyo and almost the whole of Yokohama were destroyed.

The earthquake had occurred just when the housewives were fanning into a blaze the charcoal in their cooking *hibachi* in preparation for the midday meal. The shocks brought down the flimsy wood and paper buildings and soon huge fires were sweeping through the cities. Some of the sounder brick and concrete structures survived, but many, even of the more modern buildings, were gutted. Much of the old Tokyo had gone. Twenty years later the world had become inured to such horrors, but in the 1920s man had not yet learned to rival the resourceful ferocity of nature.

In Central and Western Japan the shocks were comparatively mild. Nevertheless, nearly every day for some months afterwards Nagoya experienced tremors which set the lamps swinging and the timbers creaking in the houses. For some nights after the first shock, people remained on the alert, ready to rush out of their houses if the oscillations became wide. We became sensitive to any structural movements. Thus, whenever during that autumn and winter the house was struck by a powerful gust of wind, our eyes turned instinctively to the electric ceiling lamps to see if they had been set swinging. Most of the shocks were horizontal, but once when I was in the bathtub there was a violent vertical shock which half emptied it. By this time my interest in earthquakes as an exotic curiosity had completely evaporated. Seventeen years later, during air raids on London, I compared them with my memory of the earthquake, and came to the conclusion that, on the whole, earthquakes were more frightening than bombing.

During the weeks immediately after the first shocks, the people of Nagoya were occupied in discovering the fate of relatives, friends and colleagues in Kanto. They offered hospitality to those who had escaped. One of the most pathetic cases that came to my notice was that of a White Russian family. After the Bolshevik Revolution they had taken refuge in Tokyo and now, for a second time in a few years, they had lost their home and all their belongings.

This family stood out in sharp contrast to the rest of the foreign community – about fifty of us – which consisted chiefly of American, Canadian and British missionaries, teachers and engineers. The Russians were intelligent, lively and very good company. Despite all the blows of fortune which they had sustained, they were remarkably optimistic about the future, and believed that it would not be long before their properties in Russia would be restored to them. The more conventional members of the Anglo-Saxon community were inclined to be shocked by their lack of practical judgement and their insouciance. Just before Christmas 1923 we had a whip-round, and a sufficient sum of money was collected from the members of the foreign community to enable the Russians to enjoy a reasonably happy festival. They were so grateful that they at once went out and bought handsome presents for all who had contributed. In the end they were probably out of pocket, yet no doubt their hearts were lighter.

Once the Japanese had recovered from the paralysing effects of the catastrophe, they set about grappling with the problems that ensued. Six months after the Great Earthquake, however, there was another series of shocks which destroyed many of the new temporary structures. Although this second blow plunged them into despair, the mood did not last long and reconstruction soon began in earnest. I then gained my first insight into the vigour and resourcefulness of the Japanese when confronted with disaster. Nor did all their efforts proceed from the centre. Throughout Japan, local associations busied themselves with attempts to help the refugees and to promote the work of reconstruction. I noted that the women in the provincial towns and villages lost no time in collecting together relief supplies and in sending or taking them to Tokyo. Money was raised by functional or local groups. I was expected to contribute to the College fund, to the village fund, and to funds raised by any other group of which I was a member. These vigorous reactions to trouble foreshadowed Japan's resurgence after the even greater destruction of the Second World War, when every city except Kyoto was destroyed.

The Americans showed their usual generosity by dispatching large quantities of relief supplies to Japan. Unfortunately their attempts to help were sometimes misguided. In those days the diet of the Japanese people had not been modified by Western influences to the same extent as at present. Many foods in common consumption in the Western world were unpalatable to the people, especially cheese. It can be well understood, therefore, that the authorities were embarrassed by the arrival of massive quantities of food of a kind that the Japanese could not be persuaded to eat, even when they were hungry. They pressed those who liked such food to take it off their hands. As a result, foreign households, including my own, lived for some time off these lavish supplies that were intended for the unfortunate. It may be difficult for present-day Japanese, who are accustomed to eat all kinds of foods formerly considered repulsive, to understand their forefathers' rejection of some part of the American bounty.

The reconstruction of Tokyo and Yokohama went ahead very rapidly. The flimsy houses of the old cities were replaced by still flimsier successors, and a large number of temporary structures were put up to serve as business premises. By the autumn of 1924, a year after the Earthquake, the appearance of much of Tokyo was not strikingly different to the casual observer from what it had been in 1923. During the next decade many large buildings in concrete were erected to house commercial firms, banks and public offices, and a few blocks of flats (usually with Japanese-style rooms) were put up. The majority of the citizens, however, continued to live in small wooden houses of the old style. Nearly all of these were supplied with electric light and many had gas and a piped water supply. Other services, however, considered essential in Western cities were still lacking. Even today the system of sewage disposal remains primitive in many parts of Tokyo. The visitor to the capital, or to any other Japanese city in the 1930s, was surprised at the lack of structural uniformity even in the main thoroughfares. Small wooden houses stood side by side with large modern concrete buildings. The streets were ill-made and most of them were without pavements.

Tokyo, as it developed during the two decades after the Earthquake, was again destroyed during the Second World War. Thus, during the half-century of my acquaintance with Japan, I have seen six Tokyos: the pre-Earthquake city; the city after its preliminary reconstruction; the city of the 1930s after the temporary buildings had been in large part replaced by more permanent structures; the city as it emerged from the reconstruction period immediately after the Second World War; the post-Olympic Tokyo with wide, elevated highways; and the contemporary city studded with high-rise buildings. Yet even in the present city the majority of the population is accommodated in tiny houses and is still ill-supplied with certain public services. Although wood has largely been replaced by concrete or plaster-board and paper by glass, the general appearance of some residential districts still brings to mind the scene I had observed more than half a century before.

The interiors of the houses have changed more than their outside appearance. Most of the houses have some *tatami*-covered rooms, but modern furnishings and carpeted floors have become common. The *hibachi* as a means of warming a house has been superseded by electric fires. The *kotatsu*, a charcoal stove sunk in the floor and covered with a mattress on which one used to crouch in winter, has been transformed into a kind of shallow well. One now sits on the edge of it and feet and legs are kept warm by an electric radiator fitted below. For cooking the housewife no longer depends on a clay charcoal stove. She has a gas or electric cooker

Disaster and Discord

as well as an automatic rice-boiler, a refrigerator, washing machine and all the household gadgets familiar in the West. Air-conditioning has made life in the hot and humid summers far more bearable than in my time. This has meant that the paper fan, once used everywhere and by everyone in the summer, is now rarely seen.

This change has removed a picturesque feature from the life of the streets and households. In the 1920s and 1930s fans were in constant use by both men and women during the hot weather. My fellow-lecturers and I took them with us into the lecture rooms. People in trams and trains used them. I remember an incident from the summer of 1936. I was looking out from the deck of a ship as it drew near to its berth at Yokohama. The light summer *kimono* of the welcoming crowd on the quayside looked gay enough, but it was the movements among them that held my attention. Countless coloured paper fans fluttered rhythmically like the waves of a river dancing in the sunlight. Today one's reception at Haneda Airport may be as warm, but the brightness has fallen from the air.

The Earthquake had only a short-lived effect on morale. In the early and middle twenties the outlook of the people was, on the whole, optimistic, and the political sentiments of those who took an interest either in international or in domestic public affairs were liberal. Economically, politically and culturally the Japanese were coming to terms with the Western world and, although there were some financial difficulties, the country's material progress seemed well assured. At that time the influence of the military cliques seemed to be waning, for the victory of the Allied Powers in the War had strengthened democratic tendencies. Although the government was still in the hands of an oligarchy, the influence of the political parties was growing. It seemed reasonable to suppose that Japan would gradually proceed by way of a senatorial system of government towards a parliamentary system which would correspond to that established in the Western democracies.

The young, especially those who had received a higher

education, were much attracted to what they knew of the American way of life, although this did not mean that they were uncritical of United States' policy. Others flirted with Marxism. There were occasionally outbursts of political fanaticism on the part of reactionaries, and acts of brutality by the police towards those suspected of communist or socialist ideas sometimes came to light. Nonetheless, in general, the power of the state was not used oppressively towards individuals. Indeed, where there was intolerance or oppression, it usually proceeded from the application of rigid social conventions rather than from acts of the executive towards the subject or of the employer towards the worker. It was necessary for a Westerner to remember that the Japanese had been nursed in a very different political tradition from that of Europe and were willing to accept restraints on personal freedom that would have seemed intolerable to the British or Americans.

The Japanese were trained hard in patriotism, and as their pride in their nation was very strong, they were sensitive to slights from outside. This was brought very clearly to my notice in 1924 when the United States Immigration Act was passed. As I mentioned in Chapter III, the Act abolished the arrangements which had allowed limited Japanese immigration into the United States and it put the Japanese into the same category as other Asian nationals. This was considered an insult. Japan, it was thought, had joined the ranks of the World Powers and deserved treatment consonant with its newly won position.

The irony was that it had virtually no practical effect, since the immigration of Japanese into the United States had long before been reduced to a trickle. The Immigration Act led to some revival in the popularity of the militarist and xenophobic cliques but, on the whole, the liberal trend in policy and thought persisted until the World Depression that began in 1929. Then, the worsening of relations with China, which coincided with the economic collapse and the impoverishment of the peasantry, discredited the political parties and their business supporters. Autocratic govern-

Disaster and Discord

ments, largely subservient to the militarists or the extreme nationalists, came into power.

When I paid my second visit to Japan in the summer and autumn of 1936 in order to carry out some research into recent economic developments, the political atmosphere was very different from that which prevailed in the 1920s. In the previous February there had been a revolt of young officers and other extremists against the government which, they thought, was trying to restrain the ambitions of the army in its ventures in North China and Manchuria. The Finance Minister and several other Ministers had been assassinated before the mutiny was put down. The very hotel where I lived for most of the time during this visit had been occupied by the mutineers a few months before.

It was easy to detect the tension and uneasiness beneath the façade of good manners. I found that there were many Japanese who were opposed to the extravagant assertions of imperialist claims and were distressed at the overthrow of parliamentary institutions and the discrediting of liberal ideals. "We call it the tomb of democracy," said a friend ruefully, as he pointed out the new parliament building.

The business world was obviously alarmed at the growing power of the military cliques and the extreme nationalists. Several businessmen with whom I made contact expressed indignation at the arrogance of the army and fear about the course on which Japan was being led. Some felt that their lives were threatened. Others, however, were obviously ready to come to terms with the new order. An official of Mitsui, which earlier had been one of the chief targets of the fanatics, told me that events had revealed to the business community the errors of their ways. In future, their policies must be brought into accord with that of Japan's national interests.

In 1936 Japan was being drawn steadily into the orbit of the Axis powers and her conflict with China was about to move to another stage. Government control was being extended over industry in order to promote the development of *jun-senji keizai* (quasi wartime economy). Foreign investigations into Japanese affairs were being regarded with suspicion.

In these circumstances it was surprising that so much help was extended to me in my own enquiries. It is true that I had friends in the Japanese Foreign Office who could vouch for me, while Mr Tanzan Ishibashi of the *Toyo Keizai* (Oriental Economist) and his colleagues cooperated whole-heartedly in the research. I also had connections with my former colleagues and students at Nagoya. Nevertheless, the extent of the help I received shows that the suspicions raised by the militarists were not shared by the whole country. Many Japanese were still well disposed towards Britain and America and welcomed disinterested enquiries into their affairs. Even when they were not without suspicions, they were inclined to give me the benefit of the doubt. I remember a leading cotton-spinner who, on hearing that I held a Chair at Liverpool University, wondered if I were not an agent of the Lancashire cotton industry. He nevertheless dismissed his fears and spent some hours answering my detailed enquiries about his industry. This and other experiences of the same kind were an indication, I thought at the time, that the Japanese were disposed to be hospitable and generous to strangers unless there were overwhelming reasons why they should not be.

I did not escape altogether from this fog of suspicion, although on many occasions I was unaware of the scrutiny to which I was being subjected. I have already mentioned the enquiries made by the police of my hosts at Nagoya. The suspicion did not stop at that point. A Japanese academic friend afterwards told me that one of my former colleagues had opposed any suggestion that the College should help me with introductions and information, but these suspicions were brushed aside by members of the staff who knew me better. In Osaka there was another incident which illustrated the temper of the times. During the mid-1930s a popular subject with journalists was what was called *Nihonjin no Seishin* (the Japanese Spirit); a good deal space in the newspapers was devoted to lauding Japan's unique character and her superiority to other nations. A young editor of a journal concerned with social affairs called on me at my hotel and expounded this subject at length. Finally, he asked me to tell him about *Eikokujin no Seishin* (the English Spirit). By this time I was bored by the subject and I said that I doubted whether there was one. He seemed so bewildered by my frivolous reply that I felt obliged to do my best to give him some notion of what I imagined to be the outstanding qualities of the British character.

Unknown to us, the police had observed our meeting. They followed the editor back to his office and demanded a detailed report of our conversation. A few weeks later he wrote an account of it and published it in his paper. This account, as far as I could remember, bore only a slight resemblance to the actual conversation. I did not learn of this surveillance until some time afterwards. The police were very discreet. They never bothered me nor interfered with my movements.

I was naturally well aware that some sectors of industry were likely to be politically sensitive. These I was content to avoid, for I did not wish to embarrass the people who were helping me. Sometimes my attempts to be tactful had unexpected consequences. During a visit to Kansai I told those to whom I had applied for permission to visit factories that I should like to keep clear of any establishments engaged on work of military importance. I had an introduction to one of the chief Mitsui executives in Osaka. When I met him he told me that although he and his colleagues were prepared to show me anything I wanted to see, they dared not risk offending the military. "In that case," I said, "arrange for me to see textile mills or other factories that are innocuous from the point of view of security; let us keep clear of metal or engineering works."

To my astonishment, in the course of this visit, I was taken over metal works, engineering factories and a shipyard, but not a single textile mill. I have never been sure whether this paradoxical result of my effort to be tactful occurred because it was thought that I was disingenuous in putting forward my suggestions about the factory visits, or because my hosts felt that they would be lacking in courtesy if they steered me away from certain industries for the reasons that I have mentioned. It is quite likely that the latter explanation is the true one.

While I was in Tokyo, the Japanese Federation of Industries agreed to arrange for me to visit a large bicycle factory in the neighbourhood. One day I had a call from an acquaintance at the Foreign Office to say that a difficulty had arisen because the factory was partly engaged on the manufacture of products for the army and navy. It was necessary to get permission for the visit from the Admiralty and the War Office. A request for this permission had to be made through the British Embassy. Sir George Sansom, therefore, wrote for permission on my behalf to the Foreign Office, which passed on the request to the Service departments. Soon afterwards my acquaintance at the Foreign Office rang me up in some embarrassment to say that while permission had been given, the two Service departments had named different days for my visit. He suggested that I should ask the British Embassy to write again to the Foreign Office to see if they could rearrange the visits for the same day. I wondered if all this diplomatic manoeuvring was worth while. I was inclined to drop the matter, but my acquaintance at the Foreign Office would obviously have been upset if I had done so, and the British Embassy seemed to think that it would be interesting to make another effort just to see what would happen. Ultimately the two Service Ministries gave me the permission for the same day, but they added a proviso that I must be accompanied on my tour of the factory by representatives of both the War Office and the Admiralty.

When the day arrived I turned up at the factory and had a most interesting, frank and informative talk with the owner–manager. After he had answered all my questions, he said that we had better go round the factory. I replied: "But what about the representatives of the War Office and the Admiralty who are supposed to come with me?" The manager was most indignant. He had had no word about the proviso. "In any case," he pointed out, "it is my factory and I can show round anyone I like." He was so incensed to hear of the bureaucratic suspicions with which my visit had been surrounded that he went out of his way to point to the gear-cutting that he was doing for the Admiralty and the pressings that were part of his army contracts. There was clearly nothing to hide from the standpoint of security, or at least, nothing that meant anything to me! At the end of the visit he told me that if I wanted to come again I should just turn up and he would be glad to see me. Then he drove me back to my hotel in his Austin Seven. At that time the business world – or much of it – still preserved a measure of independence and was unwilling to accept subservience to the military. Sensitive and patriotic Japanese were indignant at any lack of courtesy shown to foreign guests.

I may have been fortunate in my experience in a year of great international tension, for not everyone enjoyed such tolerance. I remember especially the treatment meted out to Morgan Young, the once famous editor of the *Japan Chronicle* (originally called the *Kobe Chronicle*). This was a daily newspaper which circulated chiefly among the foreign community in Western Japan, but was well-known throughout the Far East. Morgan Young was a first-rate journalist, a stylist and a man of courage and integrity. He wrote much of the paper himself, including its admirable leaders. The files of his paper are an indispensable source of material for students of Japan during the inter-war years. Bertrand Russell, at the time of his residence in the Far East just after the First World War, gave his opinion that the weekly *Japan Chronicle* was one of the best journals in the world.

I made contact with Morgan Young towards the end of 1923. He encouraged me to write articles for him on

Japanese economic and social affairs. Although at that time I had more confidence in my own opinions than knowledge of the subject, I certainly benefited greatly from his constructive criticisms of my hasty attempts to interpret the course of events. I had become especially interested in Japan's financial history and currency problems. At his suggestion I wrote a series of articles for his paper on Japan's Banking System which he afterwards published as a pamphlet. These received a good deal of attention, not because they had any great merit, but because so little had been written on the subject in English. I also tried to expound Keynes' ideas, as set out in his *Tract on Monetary Reform*, soon after the book appeared in the spring of 1924. Morgan Young published what I had to say, although he was obviously not convinced by my version of Keynes' thesis.

What chiefly aroused my interest at that time, however, was the relation between the price level in Japan and the rate of exchange. The country had done well out of the First World War and had accumulated, in consequence, large reserves held partly in gold and partly in dollar balances. After the collapse of the post-war boom in 1920 her current balance of payments became unfavourable, mainly because her prices moved out of line with those of her competitors. Nevertheless, she held to her policy of maintaining the exchange value of the yen and drew on her reserves to enable her to do so. In those days balance of payments figures, which are now the common coin of economic discussion, were hard to come by. Instead, students of international financial problems made use of the concept of purchasing power parity, that is, comparisons of the value of the different currencies by reference to movements in national price indices.

I did my sums and found that Japan's prices between 1920 and 1923 had remained fairly stable, while those of the United States and the United Kingdom had fallen steeply. Since the rate of exchange between the yen and the dollar had been maintained, it seemed to me that the yen had obviously become over-valued. This was damaging to the balance of payments and was the cause of the depletion of the reserves. I expounded my theme in the *Japan Chronicle* (and later in an article in the *Economic Journal*). My conclusions seemed to be justified when Japan was forced to commit her reserves to financing post-Earthquake reconstruction. The maintenance of the yen at former dollar parity then ceased to be practicable, and the rate of exchange was allowed to fall to the level that achieved a coincidence between the purchasing power parity and the rate of exchange, or as we should now say, to the level which brought the country's foreign receipts and payments into equilibrium.

If the purchasing power parity theory has blemishes, at least it helped to explain what had occurred in the early post-war years. What took me aback, however, was the criticism aroused by my articles in financial circles in Kobe once the yen had fallen. Clearly, some members of that community believed that there were no objective factors to explain the decline. One of the critics asserted that the chief cause was the uncertainty and fear roused by articles such as mine. Economists should keep their mouths shut! It may be that the general argument for such restraint is strong, but the ascription to me of any influence was, of course, nonsense, though, I suppose, flattering to my self-esteem. Anyhow, I was grateful to Morgan Young for having given me the hospitality of his columns.

In the next decade his task as an editor became much more difficult. He regarded himself as a candid friend of Japan, but his vigorous attacks on government policy in those years persuaded the Japanese that he was hostile to their country. He certainly did not allow tact to disguise his opinions. He condemned the imperialist aggression in Manchuria and North China as well as political developments within Japan itself. The thin-skinned military cliques who gradually extended their control over the country during the later 1930s reacted against his irreverent criticism of their activities. When he went on leave shortly before the outbreak of the war with China, in July 1937, they saw their opportunity. He was refused permission to return to Japan and this cost him his career as an editor in that country. His memory deserves a tribute.

VIII

Recreations, Travels and Encounters

Before I set sail in August 1922 I had been warned that I might find Nagoya a rather dull place. The old Japan hands on the ship commiserated with me. The foreign community, I was told, was very small. There were no clubs, very little sport and few other organised amusements. All this was true, and yet I was never bored during my two and a half years in Nagoya. In term time I enjoyed my work and found plenty of interesting ways of passing my leisure hours, and during the vacations I could, and did, travel far and wide.

I took advantage of the opportunity of inhabiting several worlds. There was the academic community at the College; a considerable group of other Japanese friends, business and professional; and the foreign community composed of American and Canadian missionaries and teachers, a few British engineers, two or three Germans and a White Russian family. I had an easy start, as the English colleague with whom I shared a house was already well-established when I arrived.

The Anglo-Saxon group, though diverse in its interests and outlook, formed a fairly closely-knit society. The Americans and Canadians, especially the American Consul and his wife, were generous in their hospitality. There was a tennis club. We met for excursions to the seashore, to the nearby mountains and to beauty spots in the countryside. From time to time *sukiyaki* parties in Japanese restaurants were arranged.

Appointment in Japan

The Japanese showed their characteristic curiosity about the activities of the strangers in their midst, and any happening of importance in this community was noted and discussed. Sometimes they were rather bewildered by the way we conducted ourselves. One of them expressed great surprise to hear that my friend and I, both Englishmen, had attended the celebration party on Independence Day at the American Consulate. He was even more astonished (as well he might have been) when I told him that one of the American missionaries, who came from the deep South, boycotted the celebrations at the Consulate and ostentatiously hoisted the Confederacy flag over his house. Some of the missionaries thought that I was letting the side down by attending a Buddhist service on a special occasion at the request of one of my colleagues and by subscribing to the fund raised to maintain the village shrine. However, this disapproval did not lead to any breach in our friendly relations.

The Japanese, except for those with long experience of life in the West, were not accustomed to entertaining guests to meals in their own houses and preferred to take them to restaurants. Their wives never accompanied them on such occasions. Some of them were hesitant about inviting foreigners to their houses because either they doubted whether they could make such guests comfortable or were shy of exposing the simplicity of their domestic arrangements to a supposedly critical gaze. However, I was fortunate in my Japanese friends. One of them, formerly a fellow-student, had a fine country house not far from Ashikaga in Tochigi Prefecture. During my first summer in Japan I stayed with him for a spell and delighted in the leisurely, elegant and unostentatious routine of a well-to-do household of the old style. In Nagoya itself I occasionally visited a friend who, on marriage, had been adopted into his wife's family, as it had no male heir. The couple lived with the wife's family in a fine old house with large grounds. I remember with pleasure sitting on the verandah one evening early in summer and looking on the lovely landscape garden. As night fell there came to our ears the rhythmical sound of the watchman's clappers as he made his round of the estate. I thought of the passage in Turgenev's *A Nest of Gentlefolk* about the night-watchman playing a tattoo on his board.

These friends had been educated in the West and were as much at home in a European as in a Japanese setting. I was also a frequent visitor at the house of a Shinto priest. I owed this acquaintance to the fact that his daughter was betrothed to one of my students. He and his family were well-disposed towards foreigners and anxious to do their part in relieving the loneliness from which they might suffer. One of their number had kindly recollections of the way he had been received in an American household many years ago. Occasionally a Japanese colleague from the College took me to visit a young artist who lived a somewhat Bohemian life. I recall with particular pleasure a national holiday spent at his house. We lounged on the *tatami*, talking and admiring the drawings and paintings which he set before us. We drank tea and *sake* without interruption. At irregular intervals we were served with food, and from time to time the ex-*geisha* who lived with him entertained us with music on the *koto* or *shamisen* and with lively or plaintive songs. Nowhere else in the world would it have been possible to spend a day in quite that fashion.

The only foreign-style entertainment regularly available in Nagoya was provided by the cinema. Most of the foreign films were American, but occasionally a Continental film was shown. The American films attracted large audiences since the world they disclosed to the untravelled Japanese doubtless seemed even more extraordinary than it appeared to Europeans. The audience, having discarded its *geta* at the door or having had its shoes fitted with cloth covers by the doormen, sat on the *tatami*-covered floor. Foreigners who were reputed to be too ungainly to squat elegantly were provided with bentwood chairs at the back of the hall. In an attempt to attract their custom, or perhaps simply to demonstrate a knowledge of foreign languages, the cinema managers sometimes commended their programmes and specified their terms in English. One such announcement read: "Price – First Class 1 yen, Common 60 sen. However, the soldier and the child, half." You could hardly ask for a chair if you were "common"!

Japanese audiences expected cinema performances to last as long as their own theatrical shows – usually five hours or more. The tedium of the silent films was relieved by the commentator who sat alongside the screen. He translated the English captions into Japanese and provided a dialogue from his own lively imagination, with superb imitations of the foreign voices, especially the female ones. In those days the Hollywood kissing scenes offended Japanese taste and they were cut out of the films. The commentator made up for this elision by giving the audience his own realistic interpretation of the love scenes which everyone enjoyed much more than if they had had to depend on the pictures or captions. I generally understood enough of what he was saying to appreciate the flavour of his remarks.

Now and then I attended the Kabuki theatre. I always invited a student to come with me as I could not follow the dialogue without his interpretation. Even without this, I should have been entranced by the costumes and scenery, and I could always enjoy the magnificent acting. It was at a performance of one of these plays that I first realised that the apparently passive Japanese were in fact a highly emotional people. I observed that during the more tragic scenes many of those present were in tears.

On a later visit to Japan, my wife and I were taken behind the scenes after a performance to meet one of the most renowned actors of the time, Kikugoro. He was still dressed in the magnificent robes of the part he had played and he carried himself with the air of the *daimyo* (lord) he represented. His entourage treated him with a deference to which his stage rank entitled him. In this strange environment it was easy to forget the twentieth century and imagine oneself among the heroes of old Japan. I could understand how, in Rostand's *L'Aiglon*, time and circumstance combined to half-persuade Metternich that it was the Emperor himself who lay asleep in the adjoining room.

In the 1920s the audience in a Japanese theatre sat on the *tatami*-covered floor, and each party was separated from the others by narrow raised platforms which gave access to the sitting places. During the performances attendants brought tea and other refreshments and also, in winter, little *hibachi*. These were necessary, for the theatres were otherwise unheated and cold winds blew through the cracks and joints in the wooden shutters that formed the outside walls. In winter it was wise to follow the native custom and to put on several layers of outer wear before setting out for the theatre.

On a few occasions the people of Nagoya were given a chance to see examples of the art and drama of the Western world. Once, Pavlova came to dance. Among the crowds who flocked to see her were scores of local *geisha* who watched her athletic caperings with astonishment. They said they admired the performance, but I doubt if this was the truth. On another occasion an Italian company gave a performance of *Rigoletto*. Whatever the audience thought of it, the singers obviously loathed their experience. The weather was very cold. The members of the audience, swathed in layers of padded clothing and crouching over *hibachi*, could just survive. The unfortunate singers, however, were exposed to icy draughts, and the orchestra could scarcely be identified, muffled as they were in greatcoats and scarves. The same opera company added considerably to the hilarity of the times by its performance in Tokyo of *Madam Butterfly*. Even Japanese politeness could not restrain the audience from giggling as fat Italians, with *kimono* wrongly crossed over in front, waddled across the stage in an attempt to imitate the elegant shuffling steps of Japanese ladies.

On special occasions I was taken to see *Noh* plays and dances. These performances are given on a type of stage peculiar to them. They are in no sense popular entertainments and are given before an audience of cognoscenti. The words are understood only by those who have studied the plays and, since even the slightest gestures on the part of the masked actors are of significance, a Westerner who has not been coached beforehand is left somewhat bewildered, however delighted he may be with the aesthetic charm of the scene itself. I once spent a whole Sunday at a *Noh* theatre, for the performance extended throughout the day and evening. When I withdrew exhausted, at about 6 P.M. while the performance was still continuing, the friend who had taken me wondered if I had enjoyed the experience. On this question my feelings were a little mixed. Later on I saw performances at the Peers' Club in Tokyo for which the audience had been carefully coached beforehand, and these I found magnificent and very enjoyable.

Amateurs of *Noh* form groups to rehearse the music and dances, and their performances, being more intimate, are particularly pleasing. I was once present at a *Noh* dance given by a group of amateurs in an old restaurant. After dinner a low stage was placed at one end of the room, and here the dancer gave his performance, while the rest of the group accompanied him with music and chanting.

A recurrent pleasure was given by the frequent festivals and popular plays. In the autumn there were the *kiku ningyo*, performances of puppets in costumes made of chrysanthemums. In all seasons of the year one was liable to encounter processions of Shinto priests and their excited acolytes who, shouting and chanting, pulled the sacred and richly adorned chariots through the crowds of sightseers. Such events, though exotic and entrancing to me, were commonplace to the ordinary Japanese at that time.

Now and then the College Faculty held parties in restaurants. Here I first observed what has always impressed me since, how easily the Japanese throw off their preoccupations and cares when they meet together for pleasure. Perhaps the style of domestic architecture, the cool, uncluttered rooms with finely polished woods, reed-covered mats and delicately tinted sanded walls, provides the proper environment. The method of serving meals, with each guest seated on a cushion before a low lacquered table, establishes at once an intimacy that is lost in banqueting rooms furnished in Western style. Shyness is soon banished and the most self-conscious is easily persuaded to relax. It comes to my mind that at my first College party all those present were asked to contribute a song. The Principal led off with an old Chinese love song of some duration. Unfortunately, my ear was not as yet attuned to Oriental music and my appreciation of this performance was as tepid as was his of my rendering of a chorus from the Scottish Students' Song Book.

Occasionally parties were enlivened by the presence of *geisha* who sang, danced and entertained the guests with jokes and prattle. In their elaborate coiffures and magnificent *kimono* and *obi* they were a delight to the eye, although their stylised manners and appearance made it difficult to believe that they were real people. Later on I came to appreciate more fully the ritualistic character of a *geisha* party. One in particular stands out in my memory, perhaps because it followed very faithfully a classical course.

I had been invited to a restaurant to discuss the problems of the steel industry with the director and staff of one of the leading firms. For some time after we had seated ourselves beside our little tables (I, as the honoured guest, next to the *tokonoma*), our talk was of technicalities. The *geisha*, after the first flurry of their entry, sat in silence, filling up our *sake* cups or handing us food. Then, as the protracted meal drew to its close, our interest in the steel industry waned, conversation became more general and the *geisha* began to take more part in it. Soon we had forgotten the steel industry and had begun to play the conventional parlour games which lend an element of agreeable frivolity to such a party. Then the time came for the *geisha* to draw on their repertoire of dances and songs. When these performances were over, the guests were themselves in a mood to sing, while the *geisha* prompted them and accompanied them on the *shamisen*.

The gradual progress of such a party from gravity to gaiety, in the company of cultivated friends who were quick to adapt themselves to the mood and disposition of the guests, never failed to fascinate me. I am inclined to amend Talleyrand's famous dictum about life under the *ancien régime* and to say that those who have not been present at such a party have no understanding of what is meant by *la douceur de vivre*! No doubt the experience would pall after frequent repetition.

In subsequent visits to Japan I noticed that the *geisha* have gradually adapted themselves to the changing spirit of the times. Except when they are performing a traditional dance, they wear less elaborate head-dress than formerly. They even play foreign instruments, perform modern dances and sing modern songs. They have always kept their eye on topical events and fashions and have modified their repertoire accordingly. For instance, a dance in vogue at one time was the base-ball dance in which the performers imitated the strokes and actions of the base-ball players. During the early 1950s, when Japan was suffering from a coal shortage and official propaganda was directed towards encouraging higher productivity, the *geisha* and their clients did their bit by performing the coal-miners' dance. In this the movements of the dancers were supposed to represent the actions of hewing the coal, loading the trucks and pushing them along.

Whether the *geisha* herself finds the repetition of the ritual boring is not for me to say, but this question can be asked of any professional entertainer in West or East. The exhibition of accomplishment in dance and song and the renown which some of them acquire may compensate for the toils of the career. Some *geisha* make good marriages and others, after retirement, use their savings for establishing restaurants. When a *geisha* is launched on her career she assumes a stage name which may sometimes be passed on to worthy successors. Sometimes the succession runs in the same family. A Gion *geisha* told my wife that both her mother and grandmother had been her stage predecessors.

Recreations, Travels and Encounters

At one of the parties I attended in Tokyo a *geisha* informed me that she had two living predecessors, both called by her name. Her immediate predecessor had married a member of one of the *zaibatsu* families, while the first bearer of this name was the proprietress of the restaurant in which the party was being given.

I found that an admirer of her talents had written poems in her honour, so I thought I should try my hand. The following verses were the best that I could manage. I include them here, not because I have any pretensions as a versifier, but because, when the poet son of my host turned them into a Japanese poem, he paid me the compliment of saying that my lines were Japanese in feeling and went easily into his language.

Evening in Shimbashi
The petals of the evening
Fall on the mind's dark waters
Bright but languid lie
As memory sweeps them on.
Sad and sweet are her songs,
The songs of old Yamato,
And gravely gay her smile
That soothes as a caress.

O-M-san, willow in springtime,
Grace of the autumn evening,
Over her *shamisen* bending,
Strings of the *shamisen* sweeping,
Murmurs, and stays eternal
An hour of fleeting life.

On another occasion my hosts and the *geisha* thought of a charming way of interesting and entertaining me. They went the round of Japan in imagination, singing in turn the traditional songs of all the provinces. I was sorry that I could join in only two of them: *The Song of the Kiso River* and *The Song of the Isle of Sado*. Once, in the course of a party of this kind, a former student sprang to his feet and announced that he had a contribution to make. He then proceeded to sing *It's a Long Way to Tipperary*. This was the first time that I had heard the verses as well as the chorus!

I have sometimes been asked by Japanese whether I thought that the unique form of entertainment provided by the *geisha* had sufficient aesthetic value to warrant its survival in the modern world. I could answer "yes" without hesitation. Nonetheless, I have my doubts whether it will survive. *Geisha* parties are extremely expensive, and in the absence of lavish business entertainment allowances, they could scarcely have continued during the post-war period. Many young Japanese find little attraction in them and prefer the tasteless night clubs and cabarets of Western pattern which now flourish in Japan.

The changes in the position of women in society has already made the institution somewhat anachronistic. In the past it would have been unthinkable for a Japanese wife to accompany her husband to a party, and women familiar with modern trends in social ideas have for a long time strongly disapproved of *geisha*. Now the wives of Western guests are sometimes invited to accompany their husbands, and, occasionally, Japanese couples go out together, for the Japanese wife is gradually ceasing to be the honourable lady of the back room. It seems likely that if the *geisha* survives, she will be transformed from a private into a public entertainer. By tradition her services were called upon almost exclusively for the entertainment of small groups in private rooms, restaurants and tea-houses. *Geisha* have, however, occasionally given performances in theatres, and many tourists have seen their famous Cherry Dance in spring at Kyoto. At the *geisha* school in that city, moreover, there is a theatre where the Gion give public performances from time to time to large audiences. This points the way to future developments.

From the beginning I was entranced by the beauty and calm atmosphere of the old-style Japanese restaurants, but for some time my pleasure in them was qualified by the fact that I found much of the food unpalatable. It was a delight to the eye, but unwelcome to my palate. Nowadays I like it very much. It has the additional advantage of being very easy to digest. Perhaps, as a young Japanese who prefers Western food said to me recently, "Japanese food is food for the old." At any rate, it took me a year or so to learn to appreciate authentic Japanese cuisine, although, like all foreigners, I enjoyed at once the sort of dishes that have been influenced by foreign contacts, such as *tempura* or *sukiyaki*. A few months after my arrival I was taken by a Japanese friend to a restaurant of high standing and I was asked what Japanese dish I preferred. I replied: "*Oyako domburi*", which immediately drew chuckles of embarrassment from my host and the waitress. This dish is a bowl of rice, chicken and egg, and is regarded as homely, if not plebeian; hardly the thing for the chef of a high-class restaurant. I had evidently committed the same kind of fault as the Prince of Wales had done over the coolie costume.

One of the attractions of eating out in Japan lies in the wide variety of restaurants. Nowhere else has imagination been so successfully applied in providing an appropriate environment for the kind of meals that are served. Some restaurants of old Japanese style consist of a series of elegant rooms modelled on the most admired architectural standards of the past with an outlook on to a landscape garden. Others aim deliberately at a rough simplicity. A few yards from the Ginza there used to be a small restaurant which tried to reproduce the atmosphere of a hunting lodge, austere rooms with crude woodwork, where steaks were cooked before the guests on a charcoal brazier. "This is hunting cook," my friend informed me. In a fashionable part of Tokyo one can still find a restaurant built and equipped like a farmhouse, with farm implements hanging on the walls. There are many tiny restaurants which serve raw fish and rice or skewered meat at counters behind which the food is prepared.

In Nagoya I have dined at a restaurant which specialised in *Nagasaki-ryori*, sea food which owed much to Dutch

Appointment in Japan

influence, and where models of old ships and an artificial stream flowing beside the corridors supplied an appropriate setting. Such restaurants are, and always were, expensive. In my early days I naturally patronised simpler places. For instance, I occasionally had meals in Buddhist temples. They consisted of various kinds of roots and vegetables. The taste was interesting and the meals succulent, but not so nourishing as to impair one's spiritual powers. Occasionally I went to a little restaurant which advertised in English "Ham and Eggs". There, if one only wanted ham, one had to order: "ham and eggs, *tamago nashi*" (ham and eggs without eggs).

In my early days there were comparatively few restaurants which served Western food, at any rate in the provinces. During the 1930s, however, their numbers increased, and in Tokyo many tea-rooms and cafés made their appearance. Of these one of the most interesting was the Ruskin Tea Room on the Ginza. This was a favourite resort of students. It was run by a member of the Mikimoto family, the famous producers of cultured pearls. He was an admirer of Ruskin and the tea-room was furnished in Victorian style and displayed manuscripts and letters relating to Ruskin, and pictures of Coniston. Its chimney-piece was probably the last one I ever saw draped in fringed velvet!

I was rather surprised and much amused to find that, although alcohol does not suit the Japanese, most of whom soon show signs of its effect, they are very tolerant of those who become tipsy. Indeed, heavy drinkers seem to be admired. One of the most popular scenes in the Kabuki theatre is that in which Benkei, the bluff and trusty henchman of Yoshitsune, gets drunk by imbibing large quantities of *sake* from a huge drinking bowl. In my day, one of the British mechanics employed by a Nagoya engineering firm earned the reputation of being a hard drinker. At the end of his term of service, his Japanese colleagues escorted him to his ship after a prolonged farewell celebration, and left him prostrate on his berth.

When one of them described this afterwards, he added with reverence: "He was a great warrior."

In the world of sport the Japanese already belonged equally to East and West. At the College some students played base-ball and tennis and others practised *judo*, *sumo*, *kendo*, or archery. The Ministry of Education encouraged athletics and on one day every year members of the staff, as well as the students, were supposed to engage in sports and games of their own choice. Some of my colleagues were only indifferent athletes, but a token participation was required from everyone. In the city itself the *sumo* contest was a notable annual event. A huge circular tent was put up in an open space, and here for several days large audiences watched the wrestlers as they strove to push each other out of the central ring. I found the Shinto ritual that preceded and accompanied the contests much more interesting than the wrestling itself. This was not the view of the people of Nagoya. The enormous wrestlers were conspicuous as they strutted about the city, with their hair dressed in an old-fashioned topknot. Everywhere they were observed with admiration and even awe.

Sometimes my students invited me to accompany them on their outings to the hills or the sea. I particularly enjoyed the occasions when I was taken to festivals held on summer nights in the harbour. Boats filled with family parties or groups of friends, and illuminated with Japanese lanterns, drifted to and fro; fireworks were let off; songs were sung and food and drink consumed at short intervals. On these occasions the Japanese people seemed full of fun and good humour. They did all they could to help the foreigner in their midst to share in their enjoyment and they offered him little presents of sweetmeats, or *nori* which went well with the *sake*.

I also went further afield, for example, to see the cormorant fishing at Gifu, which is now a well-known tourist attraction. Once I joined a party which had hired a boat to shoot the rapids on the Kiso river. This was really exciting. The boatmen pushed their stoutly-built craft from the shore at a point where the current was running strongly. Soon we were rushing down the river while the boatman steered us with long poles away from the rocks strewn plentifully over the river bed. Since the stream is wide, one is not conscious of speed until the boat approaches a rock and that moment is indeed thrilling. I was never quite sure whether this was really a dangerous sport or not. The boatmen controlled their craft with confident skill, but if we had hit a rock in the midst of the raging torrent, I would not have given much for our chances.

During the summer vacation of 1923, before the Earthquake, I spent several weeks at Chuzenji, a lakeside resort in the mountains above Nikko. Today a motor road runs from Nikko to Chuzenji and far beyond. At the time of my first visit the road went only half the distance, to a place called Umagaeshi. After that there was a steep track which wound up the mountains. I persuaded two rickshaw men to deal with my luggage and I myself walked, leaping aside from time to time as the pack-horses we met took bites at me. Japanese horses were nearly all xenophobic and never lost an opportunity of making themselves disagreeable to foreign passers-by. As I felt grateful to the rickshaw men for their hard pull, I paid them well and earned exceptionally low obeisances and prolonged thanks. A fellow guest at the Lakeside Hotel where I stayed, an old hand who had observed the transaction with disapproval, said to me as I entered the vestibule: "I see that you have overpaid them."

In those days Chuzenji was an enchanting place, a quiet, beautiful lake with tree-covered mountains rising above it. The village was composed of a few simple hotels (including one in foreign style) and a number of villas tenanted for the most part by members of the diplomatic corps, of whom the most famous at that time was the French Ambassador, Paul Claudel. A few shrines and temples nestled in the trees. There were foresters' huts and wood-yards on the lowest slopes of the hills. It was in this neighbourhood that I saw woodmen sawing a tree into planks by methods identical to those shown on the celebrated Hokusai print.

A visitor found mountain walks extending in all directions. If he climbed to a pass on the south side he could see, far off in the valley, the old copper-mining district of Ashio. From the opposite end of the lake he could make his way across the *Sinjo Gahara* plateau, rich with azaleas and lilies, to Yumoto, a hot-spring centre, or he could accompany the white-clad pilgrims as they set out at nightfall to climb the nearby mountain, Nantai-san. Each of them carried a paper lantern, and watchers gathered below to see the lights winding up through the trees. There was good sailing on the lake, and I spent many hours rowing to further shores and to the islands. The waters of Lake Chuzenji flow out over the famous Kegon Falls, at one time favoured by desperate lovers intent upon committing suicide. They seemed far from grim when I first saw them, for it was the time of the summer festival. In the evening, paper lanterns were lit and placed on little rafts on the lake. As the current gathered force they were drawn to the falls and the lights extinguished as they plunged below.

All this area has now been developed into a large tourist resort and I hardly recognised it on my last visit. A motor road runs past Chuzenji to Yumoto and far beyond into the mountains. A visitor to the Kegon Falls used to clamber down the rocks to the foot of the cliff from where he could observe, in isolation from the world, the whole extent of the waterfall. On my last visit I queued for a place in a lift. A notice at the entrance warned me to beware of pickpockets.

During the next summer vacation in 1924 I spent about a month at Karuizawa, another mountain resort much favoured by foreigners. Karuizawa offered plenty of opportunities for amusement. There were tennis, amateur theatricals, concerts and dancing. In the neighbourhood was the great volcano Asama. This I climbed in the late evening in company with a large party of pilgrims who had gathered from all parts of Japan. At midnight we reached the summit and looked down into the glowing crater. Asama was irritated at our impertinence and at that moment there was an earthquake which caused us to make a quick descent. A few weeks later Asama was sprinkling the countryside with fine, white ash.

From Karuizawa I set out with two language officers from the British Embassy, on a walking tour in the Japan Alps. For days we walked over high passes, climbed mountains and cliffs and waded up rivers. Our leader who had planned the trip was a captain in the Ghurkas. His standards of accomplishment were high. He drove us on ruthlessly, ignoring our occasional protests, and always succeeded in bringing us to a lodging late in the evening when we were beginning to despair of arriving. In the hot spring mountain resorts, which we reached from time to time, we found comfortable inns and we were greeted amiably by our fellow-guests as we wallowed in the communal bath. Even in the remote places the inns, though simple, were quite clean and we had nothing worse to deal with than a few fleas. Although foreigners were a rarity and rather an embarrassment to the innkeepers, they always received us hospitably and did their best to provide enough food to satisfy our ravenous appetites. We sometimes met with vestiges of the old regime. Once we were asked, on registering at an inn, to classify ourselves as *heimin* (commoners) or *shizoku* (descendants of *Samurai*). We left it to the innkeeper, who decided that as guests coming from afar we could rank as honorary *shizoku*.

In the course of our travels we had some unexpected encounters. The oddest people, whom we met towards the end of our trip, were an American couple. They belonged to a Christian sect which regarded dancing as a necessary part of worship. As they went about Japan, they performed their religious dances wherever they could find a congregation. The more conventional missionaries, I heard, disapproved of them, but I expect that they were quite warmly received by the Japanese, since dances form an important part of their religious ritual.

In my day the Japanese-style hotels in the towns, as well as the country inns, were much cheaper and more interesting places to stay in than the foreign-style hotels, although not always as comfortable. The innkeepers usually did their best to meet the special demands of their foreign guests, who were objects of curiosity as well as of inconvenience to them. Since then there have been great changes. The first-class Japanese-style hotels today are unrivalled, for they combine the beauty and charm of old times with the comforts of the present. However, they are no longer cheap. They always depended on the presence of ample personal service. The industry of which they are part is labour-intensive in the extreme and it cannot easily save labour by substituting equipment as foreign-style hotels do. The shortage of labour and the rise in wages have, therefore, made it very difficult for innkeepers to maintain the old standards of service, and when they do so they have to charge high prices.

Even in the 1920s the Japanese loved to travel to see the famous places in their beautiful country. For those who could afford it, tours were organised by neighbourhood groups, schools and other institutions, and during the national holidays one was sure to encounter parties holding banners and streamers which showed where they had come from. This is still true, and nowadays, of course, there are far more of them. In the past many of the parties, some of whom travelled great distances on foot, made the circuit of the chief shrines and temples and paid their obeisances to the gods. They had their cards stamped with the names of the sanctuaries and beauty spots and left their prayers and wishes hanging in paper strips at the shrines, and returned with amulets that would bring them good luck and longevity. The students loved walking tours in the mountains, and when I met a group of them in the course of my own excursions, I was often astonished to hear of the distances they claimed to have covered. Today the stream of tourists and visitors has become a great flood. Coaches pour out of the cities for destinations far and near, for Japan has been enjoying a leisure boom. The once lonely mountains have been made accessible by motor roads and cable railways.

The curse of modern tourism, which destroys what it is

organised to admire, is especially obvious in Japan because so much of its beauty, both natural and man-made, is intimate and delicate. The temples, shrines and gardens made their appeal in a quiet and lonely hour. Their charm and tenderness evaporate in the presence of noise and multitudes. The structure of the fragile buildings cannot sustain the tread of thousands. When I was first in Kyoto (and subsequently I took every possible opportunity of revisiting it) I found my way to the Ginkaku-ji. I sat enthralled in a wooden pavilion that overlooked the rocks, streams, mosses and raked sand of the garden. Today access to the pavilion is barred and, except in the early hours of the morning, the genius of the garden has hidden himself from the admiring crowds. In the holiday period the main streets of Kyoto are lined with coaches which have brought school-children from all over the country to view the national treasure house. Before Japan became rich, most of them could not have afforded to come except, perhaps, once in a lifetime. Only the fortunate could then enjoy what Kyoto had to offer. Alas, that offering is no longer what it was fifty years ago.

It is a matter of regret that opportunities of seeing China during my time in the Far East were few. One visit, however, stands out sharply in my memory. In the spring of 1925 I went to stay with a friend, C. A. Ashley, who was then living in Shanghai. He and I decided to spend a few days at Hangchow, the famous beauty resort about 120 miles to the south-west. It was a time of civil war and the contending armies were engaged on the boundaries of Shanghai. The International Settlement and the French Concession were surrounded by barriers of barbed wire and sandbags, and were guarded by troops. There were, however, no restrictions on foreign excursionists, so one evening we caught a train for Hangchow.

There were no other passengers in our carriage when we started, but when our train made its first stop beyond the boundaries of the International Settlement, it was boarded by heavily armed soldiers. They paid little attention to us, although we became slightly uneasy when some of them began to squint down the sights of their rifles and to click the locks. We were served with dinner by the car attendants, who were unperturbed by the invasion. Presently the troops disembarked from the train as suddenly as they had boarded it, but from then on our progress was slow. We later discovered that this was because the rival army was in retreat over the territory through which we were travelling and that it had partly destroyed a bridge that lay between us and our destination. The train driver evidently decided to take a risk and we gingerly crossed over. A detachment of the opposing army then boarded the train and enjoyed a free ride for a few miles.

We arrived at Hangchow four or five hours late. It was by then about two o'clock in the morning. The hotel where we had reserved rooms had given us up, and there was no one to meet us, so we climbed into rickshaws and, having no word of the language, surrendered ourselves to the coolies. The ride was most strange and romantic. We were borne through the completely deserted, silent, dimly lit streets of the city without any notion of where we might end up. Ultimately we were deposited at a hotel of modest construction, though not the one at which we had made reservations. We were given fine large rooms overlooking the lake which is the glory of Hangchow. We found, however, that although every room had its private bathroom, there was no plumbing. The hotel company had run out of funds before the installation was completed. When, in the morning, I demanded a bath, I was led to a stiflingly hot outhouse where I found a tub and a large pan of water boiling on a charcoal stove. The hotel people were doubtful of their capacity to provide us with breakfast, but the boy of an English BAT representative presented himself and served us with an excellent meal, having drawn on his master's supplies. When in the evening his master himself put in an appearance and invited us to dine with him, it was obvious that he was quite unaware that his boy had already entertained us.

Appointment in Japan

In the Far East it is as well to float with the tide and, in conformity with this principle, we allowed ourselves, on quitting the hotel on the morning after our arrival, to be ushered by one of the staff into a little boat. Then began one of the most delightful days of my life. The lake of Hangchow is dotted with little islands on which are to be found temples, pagodas and restaurants. We could not speak to our boatman, but we let him paddle us from island to island at his will. The beauties of the lake are enhanced by the names given to its main features; some of these names we afterwards learned. My memory of the physical details has grown dim, but such names as the Island of the Three Pools and the Moon's Reflection recall the enchantments of long ago, which even the Marxist-Leninist vocabulary of present-day China has not thrust into oblivion.

At midday our boatman brought us to an island restaurant where we seemed to be the sole guests. Vast bowls of food were set before us as we sat in a cool, artificial grotto in the garden; what was left after we had had our fill was enough to sustain the staff for several days. At the end of the meal a gardener appeared, and it was he who served us with tea. We did not lack occasional company in the course of this stay in Hangchow. Now and then people stopped us and shook hands. A few liked to practise their English. They seemed anxious that we should miss nothing worth seeing. Once our sleeves were plucked and we were invited down a dark alley. Although fearful we should find ourselves in a brothel, it turned out to be a deserted mosque and we were invited especially to admire its baths. On another occasion we were led to a heap of rubble which was all that remained of an ancient pagoda. Its collapse a few months earlier had been caused by tourists who for years past had chipped pieces of stone from the base for souvenirs.

From time to time as we wandered about the neighbouring country we came across companies of soldiers drilling or manoeuvring. Both the armies seemed to be in the neighbourhood, to judge from the uniforms. But there was

Recreations, Travels and Encounters

no fighting and they seemed to take no interest in us. In fact, the indifference of most of the Chinese to the presence of foreigners among them stood out in sharp contrast to the inquisitiveness of the Japanese. The impression I carried away with me from China was that of leisurely activity pursued against a background of immense disorder. To arrive back in Japan was to return to urgency and purpose – and curiosity.

IX

Economic Progress and Social Development

I have written elsewhere of Japan's economic development in the modern era, and I am not here concerned with any systematic description or analysis of her achievements. Yet my reminiscences would be incomplete if I failed to make further reference to my impressions of the country's economy during the 1920s and to the changes that I found on subsequent visits.

When I arrived in 1922, Japan was a country of peasant agriculture and small workshops with a fringe of large-scale manufacturing industry. Much of what we now call the infrastructure was already well developed. She had an efficient mercantile marine, railway system and postal and telegraph services. Most of the towns had electric trams, but motor traffic hardly existed and local transport depended on bicycles, rickshaws, oxcarts and horse-drawn vehicles. The use of electricity for lighting and traction was widespread. There was a modern banking system, the structure of which recalled that of Britain in the middle of the nineteenth century before the consolidation movement began. The government, from the beginning of the modern era, had realised the importance of education, and for many years a comparatively high proportion of the national income had been spent on schools and colleges.

One of the outstanding features of the economy was the *zaibatsu* – the great business houses. We should now call these conglomerates, for their ramifications extended to finance and trade as well as to most branches of the manufacturing and mining industry. Yet, although large establishments were found in shipbuilding, engineering, cotton- spinning, pottery and mining, the output of these industries was still comparatively small. The only industries which rivalled those of the West were textiles. The number of workers in factories with five or more employees was well under two million, and over half this factory labour force consisted of women.

I have already described how, when I walked about Nagoya and the nearby countryside, I saw at every turn examples of the little workshops where the greater part of the country's manufacturing industry was being carried on. On a visit to Kiryu in Tochigi Prefecture, I saw establishments representative of the silk-reeling industry which produced about two-fifths of the country's exports. The streets were lined with small mills. Artificial channels had been cut down each side and the flowing water supplied the power for the machines. I was told that electric motors were just beginning to displace the water wheel.

I paid visits to some of the textile mills, both large and small. Most of the larger establishments had dwelling quarters attached to them where the girls who made up the larger part of the labour force were housed and boarded. This was a feature of Japanese industry, and has often been described. I was told that at that time the women workers received wages of from one yen to one yen fifty sen a day (say, 10–15 pence); much of this was sent to their families or saved up for dowries. I noticed that the employees were packed in tightly, sometimes ten girls to a small sleeping room, but the accommodation was very clean. In addition, many of the factories I visited had study and lecture rooms and educational courses were provided by the management.

If Japan in the early 1920s bore many of the marks of an underdeveloped country, it was obvious even then that the rate of change was rapid. During the two and a half years I was in Nagoya large areas of the town were transformed.

New wide roads were cut; the tram services were extended to the growing suburbs; several large blocks of offices and a number of modern factories were erected or extended, and taxi-cabs appeared at the railway station. I became even more conscious of how fast Japan was moving when I returned to England in 1925. I remember that I was surprised, and even rather dismayed, to find the places I knew almost exactly as I had left them. In the late 1920s the pace of change quickened. Several new hydro-electric stations were built to exploit the country's reserves of water power, and the manufacturing industry expanded and widened its scope. In other respects life was changing. I have before me a letter from a former student written at that time in which he remarks that: "*jin*-rickshaw is decreasing and one-yen taxi is replacing it, paper-covered *shoji* are being replaced by glass and new *departo* are appearing in the main streets".

The World Depression of 1929–31 had a catastrophic effect on Japan, for it struck down the two great industries on which her exports depended, namely raw silk and cotton textiles. The agricultural community, which was the source of the raw silk and which provided most of the women labour for the textile mills, was especially hard hit. Prices fell steeply and this was followed by a reduction in wages and the elimination of inefficient firms.

The depression was comparatively short-lived. Recovery, which was well in train by 1933, was brought about largely by an expansionist monetary policy and improvements in industrial productivity. When I paid my second visit to Japan in 1936, I was soon made conscious that she had moved on to a new plane economically. She had become increasingly at home with modern techniques, and her growing industrial competence was demonstrated by the wider range of her manufactures. In the early and middle 1920s she had depended on foreign staffs of designers, engineers and technicians to initiate her infant aircraft industry. By the end of the 1930s she was building efficient military aircraft to her own designs. Similarly, in the 1920s she had relied on foreign suppliers for a great deal of the power station equipment which she needed. By the mid-1930s she could produce most of the plant she required in her own factories. She had extended the range of her textiles to include rayon and wool manufactures, and had become an efficient producer of many kinds of chemicals, especially chemical fertilisers. She was unique in being the only industrial country which had actually increased the volume of export trade during the 1930s, and her rate of economic growth, at well over 4 per cent a year, was far greater than that of any other country.

This progress had been achieved partly because deflation brought down costs during the depression period and partly because, after 1932, the government successfully practised an expansionist policy. In 1936 I was astonished at the low level of prices. I found that the rent of my former house, which had been 35 yen a month in 1925, had fallen to 25 yen. In the cheap stores I bought cotton socks for 1p a pair, and a necktie for ½p. A cotton *yukata*, large enough for a foreigner, cost only 11p at a high-class shop. A rayon *obi*, ten feet in length and embroidered, was priced at 21p wholesale. Real wages had fallen, especially those of women textile operatives. The constant stream of workers from the overpopulated countryside in search of urban employment was tending to depress wages in all small-scale industries and made the price of services exceptionally low. In fact, the rise in the gross national product had not been accompanied by corresponding improvements in the standard of living of the mass of the people. It had been devoted mainly to increasing Japan's military strength and investing in strategic industries in Japan proper and Manchukuo. Some of it had been absorbed in maintaining the increased population and by the effects of the worsened terms of trade.

In many trades competition had become very fierce. To the casual visitor this was most evident in the Tokyo taxi service. The standard fare for a ride in that city was 3p, but Japanese customers were hard bargainers and often drove the price down still lower for short journeys. The competitive nature of the market was once demonstrated to me most impressively. I came out of a cinema into a drenching downpour to find that there was a rush for taxis. The drivers who were plying for hire outside the cinema responded to the increase in demand by doubling or sometimes trebling their fares. I waited. As the rain began to die away and as more taxis appeared, the fares gradually fell. By the time the rain was over they had returned to 3p. Many taxicabs in those days had two attendants, one to drive and one to spot possible customers. I found that if I halted at the side of a road several cabs were likely to make a rush for me. Presumably the cab with a spotter usually won. The spotter evidently increased the daily revenue of the cab sufficiently to cover his wage.

At the end of the Second World War Japan's industry and foreign trade were in ruins. Most of her factories and her towns had been destroyed by bombs. Agriculture, which had suffered least, for a time had to find employment for a greater number of people than ever before. However, recovery was not long delayed. From the time of the Korean War, Japan rapidly extended her industries, assisted by heavy demands from the United States forces. She imported new techniques and invested heavily in manufacturing equipment, especially in power-stations. Yet, when I visited the country in 1954, her metal and engineering industries were still high-cost producers and in technical accomplishment were far inferior to their counterparts in the West. The rate of economic growth, however, was already very high (an annual average of 10 per cent between 1950 and 1953) and by the end of the decade the economy had been transformed. Great progress had been made in most of the technically advanced industries. They now ranked with those of Western Europe. Japan had become the world's largest shipbuilder and in the production of synthetic fibres and electronic goods she was in the front rank.

In 1960 the government introduced a plan designed to

double the national income during the next decade. In the event, Japan did far better than this. The rate of economic growth in real terms continued to average about ten per cent annually, and during the quinquennium 1967–71 the increase was even faster. Her steel production, which was very small until the mid-1950s, is now second only to that of the United States. She has remained the world's chief shipbuilder. Her motor industry has risen rapidly from small beginnings, and a great petro-chemical industry has provided the basis for many new products. Her railways are among the most advanced in the world, and she has built an extensive system of trunk roads. During the last ten years her export trade has increased twice as fast as world trade as a whole.

Until the Second World War there were some grounds for the popular view that the Japanese were dependent upon Western models and that the material side of her civilisation was, as a French observer remarked, a clumsy translation. Today, she is among the pioneers of applied science and her achievements in some of the technologically advanced industries have surpassed those of Western Europe.

When I look back on the sixty years during which I have studied the Japanese economy, it seems to me that a fairly clear pattern emerges. It would be a gross exaggeration to say that the development has been consciously planned, but there has been a consistency in policy, only occasionally obscured by temporary deviations. One can conclude that, in each stage of her development, Japan has concentrated on doing some new thing superlatively well, even though this might mean neglecting for a time some aspects of the economy. When I first went to Japan, she had begun to concentrate on achieving pre-eminence in cotton textiles to support her existing superiority in raw silk and she was also rapidly enlarging her electric power capacity. During the 1930s she extended her textile base to take in rayon and wool and began to develop new branches of chemicals and engineering. In the early 1950s investment was directed into the basic industries – electric power and steel. She then proceeded to concentrate on synthetic fibres, shipbuilding and electronics, and in the 1960s on motors, petro-chemicals, transport and a wide range of technologically advanced industries. The sector of her economy most obviously neglected up to this time was housing, and it is to this and to various types of social overhead capital that much of her energy is now being directed.

This is no place for an analysis of the factors that have been responsible for the remarkable achievements of the last thirty years. I content myself with the suggestion that they can be attributed to the fortunate convergence of a number of factors favourable to economic growth, namely the presence of a large surplus rural population available for transference to modern industry; an exceptionally high rate of saving and investment and the absence of wasteful expenditure on armaments; an educational system which provided an adequate number of competent technicians, managers and skilled workers and so prepared the way for the assimilation of new techniques; and a social system congenial to rapid economic change. The circumstances in which Japan was left at the end of the War enabled her to concentrate the nation's energies on economic growth even if this meant neglecting other aims which normally preoccupy a modern state. The government took a realistic view of where Japan's interests lay and what ambitions were within her capacity.

None of this progress would have been possible without fundamental political changes. The collapse of Japanese imperialism at the end of the Second World War brought the eclipse of the groups most closely associated with it and opened the way for new men and new policies. The political, economic and social reforms initiated by the Americans during the Occupation had lasting consequences, since many of them accorded, or could be brought into accord, with what the majority of the Japanese themselves desired. The easing of many of the former restraints on personal freedom did not result in a regime of indi-

Economic Progress and Social Development

vidualism, but it played an essential part in the country's development. The country set out in a new direction. Without nostalgia for her former glories, and with imperialist ambitions cast aside, she brought all her energies to bear on economic recovery and expansion. Growth was pursued with whole-hearted enthusiasm. It was a realistic choice of goals, for many others were denied her by the circumstances of her defeat. The success that has attended the policy may be held to justify the choice.

The economic success is not now in debate, but the question is being asked whether it has not been achieved at too high a cost. The question has been posed not only by envious critics from outside but also by some Japanese themselves. It is pointed out that in housing, certain public services such as sewerage systems, and in many amenities such as the provision of parks and open spaces, Japan's achievements do not match her success in the manufacturing industry. The great cities, it is said, have become intolerably congested and noisy. The atmosphere, and the waters of lake and seashore, have been polluted; natural beauty has been ravaged in the service of material progress. These problems are common to all industrialised countries, but they have become especially urgent in Japan because of the rapidity of her economic growth and the heavy concentration of her population in a few great conurbations. The seriousness of this problem has, indeed, been much affected by the increase in numbers. When I first went to Japan the population was under 57 million. In 1970 it was 104 million – an increase of well over two-thirds. Today it stands at 115 million. More than half the population is now concentrated in the narrow belt that extends from Tokyo in the East to Osaka-Kobe in the West and comprises the regions of Kanto and Tokai. These regions together are responsible for about three-quarters of the industrial output.

The uneasiness has become widespread. A prominent banker with whom I had a conversation during a visit to Japan in the late 1960s was outspoken in his criticisms. "What is to be the end of this economic growth?" he asked.

"The pine trees on the moat of the Imperial Palace are dying in the noxious air; the birds have deserted our gardens. We are now trying to draw level with the Americans, but if that means that our cities are to become like Chicago or New York, I do not want it." Others complained that the waters of Lake Biwa and even the tides of the Inland Sea were polluted and that the fish were dying. The famous *sake*-making district near Kobe, which owed the excellence of its products to the quality of the local water, has suffered from the effluent discharged by a great steelworks nearby. (About this, however, it must be said that the steelmakers have claimed that the quality of the *sake* has improved!) I myself have long been conscious that while the Japanese are tough and resilient in character, many of the best features in their civilisation are fragile and vulnerable. I have spoken of this already in my reference to the ancient buildings. It is also true of the glories of the countryside and shores.

It is to be expected that cultivated Japanese should be troubled by these doubts about the effects of economic progress, for they are haunted by the echoes of traditional values which they left behind them when they set out on their modern career. We owe to Carmen Blacker, a percipient student of Japanese history (*The Japanese Enlightenment*), an illuminating discussion of the conceptual barriers which the Japanese had to cross in the middle of the nineteenth century in order to come to terms with Western science and technology. To a Japanese or Chinese with a conventional Confucian training, the very notion of scientific enquiry was alien and offensive. At best, scientific study was a waste of time, for it meant the neglect of the really important things. The object of civilised man should be to bring his life into harmony with the natural world of which he was part. To subject the natural world to a detached scientific examination showed a lack of reverence; it encouraged man to regard nature as "a collection of dead things, or a machine or plaything".

An immense intellectual effort was needed to escape from

the Confucian world of the mind. Imperial China, being governed by a bureaucracy trained in the classics, was too conservative to cross the gulf. It was only with difficulty that even Japan's intellectual leaders, pragmatic as they were in disposition, succeeded in doing so. If they had failed to make this jump, the modernisation of the country in the *Meiji* era would have been stultified.

Looking to the old Confucian principles as a guide to policy had been discarded long before my arrival in Japan. Indeed, I was surprised to find the educated class so ready to explore new paths. They seemed almost too susceptible to transient fashions and ideas. My students, especially, showed a thirst for notions from the outside world that was in sharp contrast to the characteristics of the typical British student. Yet in the course of my discussions with them I was sometimes pulled up short by a remark or argument which revealed that wide differences still remained between East and West. Such differences still persist among the mass of the people, but they have been rapidly diminishing in the professional, academic and bureaucratic classes.

Today Japan occupies a prominent place among the advanced nations which pay obeisance to science and to technology based on science. It is ironic that, at a time when her assimilation into this world has been completed and when she has been enjoying to the full the material advantages of the assimilation, doubts should be raised. In the West we are conscious that increases in the gross national product are not equivalent to advances in human welfare. In Japan too, the question is posed as to whether the abandonment of the old ideas is a matter for unqualified satisfaction. From the standpoint of material progress and the raising of living standards there can be little doubt about the answer. The fate of Imperial China itself underlines this conclusion, for it followed from a failure to take the measure of the new world of science and technology. Historians have pointed out that even the railways, which foreigners obtained the right to build over Chinese territory, were offensive to cherished traditions. The scars made by the railway engineers across the land and the noise and smoke from the locomotives were believed to destroy the *Feng-shui* of the places through which they passed, that is, the benevolent influences exerted by nature. This hostility was sometimes given practical expression. For instance, in the last year of the nineteenth century the Woosung Railway, built and operated by a foreign company, was purchased by the Chinese authorities who dismantled the equipment, tore up the rails and threw them into the river. This action occurred at a time when the Japanese government was vigorously promoting railway construction.

A generation ago reactionary behaviour of this sort, like the principles of the old Chinese civilisation, was held up to scorn and modern China itself has abandoned those principles. Are we so confident today in our judgements? Can we now say that the notion of *Feng-shui* should be derided?

It is chastening to reflect on the inability of men to foresee what is in store for them or the consequences of their actions. When I first went to Japan modern industry was confined to a few areas. Little was to be feared from its development and much was to be gained. With the examples of Western mistakes before them, with a smaller dependence on coal and steam power and with a less individualistic social system, the Japanese hoped to avoid many of the evils that attended the industrial revolution in the West. The far greater damage to the environment inflicted by modern technology was not foreseen.

Yet one must view this in perspective. I myself am tempted to take a personal, nostalgic view. I find difficulty in believing that any young Englishman who spends the first years of his career in the Japan of the 1980s will find the country as enthralling as I did sixty years ago. He will be more comfortable and he will escape many of the exasperations which a Western resident then experienced but he cannot experience the charm of novelty and that sense of being borne as on a magic carpet, now to the mediaeval world and now to the ancient world. I was about to add that he can no longer enjoy silence, the lost luxury of the modern age, when I remembered that, in my day, while mechanical noises were fewer and the roar of traffic unknown, the towns and villages were by no means quiet and fragrant. The tramcars screeched and even the side streets were noisy with the cries, horns, pipes and whistles of itinerant vendors, while the smell of sewage pervaded the countryside.

The present-day *Edokko* (native of downtown Tokyo) suffers exhausting journeys to work on the congested underground railway or is kept awake by the traffic on the new elevated roads. Yet his predecessor sixty years ago also had much to put up with. In busy hours passengers could be seen clinging like flies to the outside of tramcars. The life of the rickshaw coolie was usually short. Nor is the present age unique in its ravaging of nature. There are extensive regions in Japan, as in China, where the land has become barren through soil erosion caused by careless tree felling. From Otsu on Lake Biwa one can clearly see the eroded areas on the mountains from which timber was cut for the building of the Horiuji temples a thousand years ago.

Thus, we must guard against exaggerating the faults of the present by viewing them against an idealised vision of the past, although there seems no doubt that the dangers to which industrial development now exposes the country are on an altogether greater scale than ever before. While it is not easy to weigh these goods and ills, I have no hesitation in rejecting the argument that Japan's industrial growth has been bought at too high a cost in human welfare. Whatever the future may bring, the balance at present lies well in favour of modern industrialism. As I have recounted, when I first set foot in Japan, nearly half the occupied population was engaged in peasant agriculture and most of the remainder in small-scale industry and trade. The peasants lived hard and frugal lives. They had practically no machinery and few draught animals to assist them, and the farming operations depended on their prolonged and tedious labour. They had shared only modestly in the benefits that came through economic development. Many of them could not even afford to eat the rice which was their main crop and had to be content with coarser grains, such as millet. Even in comparatively good times their lot was hard. They were burdened with debt, and those who held their land on tenancy were obliged to hand over a large proportion of their produce to the landlords as rent. When the Great Depression came in 1929 they were its chief victims. Their miseries helped to breed the discontent which was a source of the reactionary movements of the 1930s and ultimately of Japan's participation in the Second World War.

The Land Reform introduced by the Occupation Authorities in the late 1940s turned the tenants into peasant proprietors and inflation wiped out their debts, but it was the rapid development of modern industry that put an end to their poverty. The demand for industrial labour led to the transference of millions of agricultural workers into industry, where they earned high and quickly rising real wages. The diminished numbers left on the land found their labour lightened and their productivity raised by extensive mechanisation. It had never occurred to me that power machines could be used economically on the tiny patches of land into which the farms were divided, and I was astounded when I first saw small tractors in operation on flooded paddy fields. In these and other ways the benefits of modern technology have been brought to the rural population.

The farmers may still not be as well off as the urban workers, but their ways of life no longer diverge as they used to in the past. Like most Japanese householders today, the farmers enjoy television sets, electric household equipment and motor vehicles. As I drove through Chiba Prefecture in the late 1960s I observed that many of the old farmhouses, though little changed in outward appearance, were equipped with solar radiation apparatus for heating. In my day the peasants and the townsmen inhabited different worlds. The contrast between ways and standards of living no longer exists.

The material results of industrial progress have accrued in

even fuller measure to the urban population. At one time workers in small-scale industry and in the service trades earned very low incomes and their productivity was also low. In 1925 I remember watching the coaling of a ship at Nagasaki. A long chain of women performed the operation by handing small roped baskets full of coal, from one to the other, between the coal stacks and the ship's bunkers. Today this process is performed mechanically, as are most of the others previously extravagant in the use of labour. The service trades and the small-scale manufacturing industries can no longer recruit labour at very low wages, because the ever-growing demand from the large-scale sector of industry has raised wages throughout the economy.

The people as a whole enjoy a better and more varied diet. They are healthier and are no longer ravaged by tuberculosis and beri-beri, a vitamin-deficiency disease formerly common. Life expectancy has risen with the growth in prosperity. Indeed, it is now one of the highest in the world. Before the war people worked very long hours in factories and workshops and in many industries they had only two free days a month. Now their hours of work in the manufacturing industry are similar to those of the West. So they have more leisure and their higher incomes enable them to enjoy it in travel and entertainment. These substantial benefits of economic growth are to be set against the losses which must also be recognised.

Old-fashioned Japanese and others to whom a concentration on material progress is distasteful, may lament the overshadowing of the older ideals of conduct. But the majority find satisfaction in the economic success of the nation and the rapid rise of their own living standards. There are, however, some signs that Japan is becoming less content than she was a few years ago with economic growth as the overriding purpose of the nation. This is, in part, because of the alarm at the damage to the natural environment caused by industrialisation and in part because affluence has brought into relief the unsatisfactory social amenities. There may be another reason. Material progress is not likely to be acceptable for long as the sole or chief national purpose of an emotional people such as the Japanese. It has been observed that the decay of the old moral codes and of traditional religion has created a vacuum which is being filled by various superstitious practices. As has happened before, several new, so-called religions have arisen and have won millions of adherents. The *Soka Gakkai*, for example, despite the vagueness of its tenets, has attracted adherents from those who have not shared proportionately in the country's economic prosperity. From this religious group there has sprung a new political party, the *Komeito*, which has won numerous seats in parliament.

How has prosperity affected the Japanese character? It is rash, perhaps impertinent, for a foreigner to attempt to reply to such a question. But since I am clear in my own mind about the answer, I shall take the risk and give it. In the 1920s there were tensions which were only half concealed by the ceremony and restraint with which the Japanese guided their conduct. They were then driving themselves hard over country still strange to them. They knew that few foreigners shared their good opinion of themselves and of their civilisation. They were aware that in some respects they were mere imitators of the West. All this gave them an inferiority complex when dealing with foreigners and made them unduly sensitive to supposed slights. Normally, their good manners concealed these tensions, but everyone who lived long in the country was conscious of them. In dealings with foreigners the Japanese often took refuge in extreme reserve which earned for them a reputation for deviousness. In their society at that time, individuals were subjected to strong pressure to conform to convention, not only to the claims of patriotism in which they had been drilled, but also to family and group obligations. Bertrand Russell, in his time in the Far East, had been struck by the contrast in their transactions with foreigners between the easy-mannered, almost indifferent,

Chinese and the tense and anxious Japanese. He may have over-stressed the contrast. I do not think that these characteristics were so obvious among the ordinary people as among those in charge of affairs and the highly educated minority.

In 1936, on my second visit to the country, the tensions had become far more acute. The authority of parliament had been overthrown and government was in the hands of an oligarchy in which the military was predominant. Japan had quarrelled with the West over the Manchurian adventure and was arming in preparation for a greater struggle. There was dissension within the country itself. Of this the February Revolt was the most obvious symptom. The business leaders and the civil bureaucracy resented the increasing dominance of the army, but were obliged to accommodate their policies to its will. The reactionaries were trying to uproot all vestiges of liberalism and frowned on the liking of the young for American ways. I have already given examples of these conflicts as I encountered them, and I need not elaborate them any further. In my view, the Japanese at that time were far more worried and unhappy than they had been in the 1920s when they were feeling their way hesitantly into a new world.

During my visits to Japan in the 1960s and later, I gained the impression that they were a happier and more relaxed, as well as a richer people. The repudiation of imperialist ambitions and the introduction of more liberal political institutions have eased the tensions which once consumed their nervous energy. At the same time, they remain patriotic and their pride in being Japanese is undimmed. They have not lost their belief that Japanese civilisation is unique – they may even exaggerate its uniqueness. It is this feeling that accounts in part for their reluctance to admit foreigners to a controlling participation in Japanese firms. They fear that foreign businessmen would understand neither the subtle relations that exist between government and industry nor the Japanese way of arriving at decisions or handling industrial relations.

However, they no longer find it necessary to assert their superiority as they once did.

The pressures exerted on individuals by the family and the group remain, but the claims are far less exacting than in the past. There is more spontaneity in social and family relationships. The change in the position of women has contributed to this. Japanese women have always been admired for their demeanour and practical capacity, but pitied by Westerners for their unequal status. Japan is still a man's world, but women now participate in professional and social life and enjoy rights previously denied them. Yet the change in their status does not seem to have robbed them of their estimable qualities. It may be that it is a good thing for women to move from subordination towards equality without ever having been the objects of chivalry.

So far the political changes of the last thirty-five years have not impaired the unity of Japanese society. They have liberated energies without destroying discipline. Indeed, the social system, as it emerged from the turmoil of the reconstruction period, seems to have been well-attuned to the policy of economic growth to which we have referred. The main question today is whether the authorities will be as successful in coping with the urgent problems of social amenity as they have been in the economic field.

X

Dai Nihon and Great Britain

In August 1922, when I embarked on the Nippon Yusen Kaisha's steamship *Suwa Maru*, bound for Kobe, my outlook on the world was very different from that of the young Englishman today who flies out of Heathrow to take up an appointment in the East. Britain was already struggling with economic difficulties which have persisted and deepened but, in those days, the difficulties were regarded as the temporary pains of adjustment to peacetime conditions. The British Empire had emerged from the War with its strength apparently renewed, for no one had yet detected the prophetic character of the settlement just reached with Ireland. Even those who questioned the methods of colonial rule (and I myself sympathised with some of the critics) stopped short of attacking its existence. It was an accepted fact. The reality and endurance of British imperial power remained the assumption of most Britons.

I was travelling on a Japanese ship, but a high proportion of the passengers were British and the shipboard arrangements were modelled on those of the P and O. After we left Marseilles, every port of call was British or British controlled: Port Said, Aden, Bombay, Colombo, Singapore and Hong Kong. Even in Shanghai, Britain's influence predominated in the International Settlement, and the presence of the magnificent Sikh police was itself an imposing demonstration of the wide extent of her power. The British business and professional men, returning from leave to their jobs in South-East Asia or China, took all this for granted. Some old China hands referred to the ominous shadow of Japanese commerce and finance and gave me as an illustration the growing importance of the Yokohama Specie Bank, Japan's semi-official foreign exchange bank and the spearhead of her enterprise abroad. Yet, except in the North of China, the British position was still unassailed. In an earlier chapter I mentioned that a young representative of a Lancashire cotton firm, who was to spend a few years in Singapore, explained to me that Japan's encroachment on the Eastern textile markets was an accident of the recent war. As soon as Lancashire's skill and enterprise were again given scope, he was confident that the markets would be recovered.

When, after my arrival in Japan, I obtained some inkling of the attitude of the Japanese towards Britain, I found that, however critical of British policy they might sometimes be, they accepted the fact of her predominance in the world. An American-trained Japanese professor of English told his students, in my hearing, that if they had command of the English language and were furnished with Bank of England notes, they could travel unhampered to any part of the world. He was, of course, even then a little out of date in regard to the banknotes. I had already been made aware of this fact when I accompanied my shipboard acquaintances to the bazaars in the ports. Some of the more knowing ones had acquired a supply of sovereigns before they sailed, and when, in the course of bargaining with the dealers, they offered to pay in these coins rather than in notes, the sterling price fell steeply.

It is difficult for a foreign resident in a country where the expression of frank opinions is no virtue to judge how his country is regarded by his hosts. I certainly received the impression that Britain still enjoyed a high reputation. Her victory in the War had surprised the numerous Japanese who had expected Germany to win and for them success was a proof of quality. The advantages to Japan of the Anglo-Japanese Alliance, only recently terminated, were

Dai Nihon and Great Britain

remembered with gratitude. As an old conservative country with a strong monarchical tradition, Britain had merits in Japanese eyes not possessed by the republics. Acquaintances who talked to me about these matters showed that they admired the long continuity of British institutions, unbroken by revolution. In casual encounters, in trains or restaurants, a foreigner was always asked his nationality. When on such occasions I said that I was British, my acquaintances seemed to become more amiable.

In her modernisation, Japan had been eclectic in her choice of models, but the status of Britain in this respect still stood high. English was the chief language of communication with the outside world and was learned by every middle-school and college student. English literature had many devotees among the university-trained Japanese, and the King's English enjoyed greater prestige than American English. The universities and high schools, for example, tended to recruit a high proportion of their foreign staff from Britain. If Americans predominated in the middle schools, this was chiefly because the missionary societies and the American YMCA paid the passage of many young teachers and so saved the Japanese Education Department a substantial expense.

In the world of commerce and finance there were many contacts with Britain, although she had long lost her predominance both as a customer and as a supplier in Japan's international trade. The chief foreign banks were British, and leading British merchant houses had well-established branches in Tokyo, Yokohama and Kobe. There were several large industrial firms jointly owned by Japanese and British, and Britain was called upon for expertise in many new ventures. Even then, however, the economic superiority of the United States was making itself felt, and Japan was turning increasingly to that country for new industrial devices. Geographically, relations with the United States were easier than with distant Britain, and American tourists were already beginning to come to Japan in considerable numbers.

Appointment in Japan

Politically the Americans were suspect. It was mainly through them that the Anglo-Japanese Alliance, once the buttress of Japan's power in the Far East, had been abrogated and, as I have already described, the Immigration Act of 1924 produced an outburst of indignation. On the other hand, American films, which were widely shown, exerted a fascination for the young Japanese. Many young people seemed to think that the representation of the American way of life bore a close identity with reality, whereas Western cinema-goers knew that it was just a form of escapism. The films did not always increase respect for Americans, or for Westerners in general. "How silly foreigners are", burst out a student in an unguarded moment after a particularly fatuous Voyage to Puerilia.

I am not sure whether the Japanese professional or businessman of those days found himself more at ease with the British in ordinary social intercourse than with other Westerners. I doubt if they detected much difference between them, although it is possible that the British reserve of manner was congenial to people who, in D.H. Lawrence's phrase, also like to "talk across a slight distance". The mass of the people hardly distinguished between the several kinds of foreigners. In my countryside walks the people I met would sometimes make comments to each other as I passed. I was as likely to hear the words *Shinajin* (Chinese) or *Chosenjin* (Korean) as to hear *Seiyojin* (Westerner). The only foreigners then known to the majority of the Japanese were Koreans and Chinese. My housekeeper was puzzled about national differences among the *Seiyojin* in Nagoya. She took a long time to get it clear that my German and Canadian colleagues and I came from different countries, or that it was not possible to travel from Europe to America by train.

There was one feature of the British tradition which surprised those of the educated classes who were aware of it. The Japanese shared with the Germans the qualities of pertinacity and application to detail. In industrial and commercial life they were essentially professionals. They had no sympathy with the British preference for the inspired amateur. Although carefree and relaxed in their leisure moments, they did not spare themselves when they were at work. A colleague told me of the favourable impression made on his countrymen by the conduct of the Germans who had been taken prisoner at Tsingtao at the beginning of the First World War. It was noticed that nearly all of them chose a subject for serious study and devoted himself to its mastery during the period of his captivity. This high seriousness earned the admiration of the Japanese.

On the other hand, German manners probably grated on the Japanese nerves even more unpleasantly than those of most other Europeans. Recently a business friend who runs one of the chief motor-component manufacturing firms in Japan gave me his impressions of the British, French and German factories which he had visited. He considered his own factories to be superior in efficiency to the French and British, but barely the equal of the German. The Germans, however, seemed to get their results by methods which the Japanese could not emulate. During his tour of a German factory, my friend observed that the manager had not hesitated to use harsh and violent language in reprimanding employees who had committed faults, and that the workmen seemed to accept these rebukes meekly. The use of such bullying tactics would have been unthinkable in Japan. My friend had obviously felt very uncomfortable during the visit.

Between the spring of 1925 when I left Japan and the summer of 1936 when I returned, the international scene had profoundly changed. Yet the British Empire still seemed secure, and Japanese businessmen were inclined to think that Britain could always find compensation in some part of her dominions for her economic troubles at home. When I was discussing the impact of Japanese competition on British industry with some officials of the Mitsui Trading Company, one of them declared, rather bitterly, that Britain *could not* lose, whatever the afflictions of particular industries. The Japanese strongly resented the charges of social dumping levelled at them by British industrialists who were suffering in their foreign markets from the competition of cheap exports from Japan. The term was, of course, meaningless and was used simply for the abuse of a successful rival. A former student of mine, then in business, said to me: "When we were taught economics at the College, we were told about the advantages to humanity of free trade and low prices; now, when we are able to produce goods cheaply and to compete, you want to restrict our trade."

Political relations between Britain and Japan had taken a turn for the worse during the 1930s because of the latter's aggression in China and Manchuria and her defiance of the League of Nations. The shift of power within Japan had had the effect of carrying her further away from the democracies and, at the time of my visit, she was already moving towards the Axis camp. It was unfortunate that in popular discussion in Britain during this period, Japan was blamed equally for her commercial success and for her military aggression. They were sometimes treated as moral equivalents, as though there were no difference in obliquity between providing the poor people of Asia with cheap goods which they were anxious to buy and imposing on some of them forms of government which they abhorred.

Nevertheless, despite all that was happening in politics, the American influence on the young at that time seemed to me to have become much stronger than it was in the 1920s. For fashions in dress and entertainment the young men and women of the cities looked increasingly to the United States. It was this corruption of ancient virtue by American example that roused the ire of the conservatives and, in particular, of the military. The new dance-halls frequented by the *moga* and *mobo* were condemned. Attempts were made to enforce codes of austerity and restraint which the young showed signs of abandoning. As war approached the restrictions on conduct were tightened. The singing of certain popular songs in tea-houses and cabarets (such as

Shima no Musume – Girl of the Island) was forbidden on the grounds that they were too erotic to accord with the dignity and virtue which should characterise the *Yamato* race.

When I paid my first visit to Japan after the Second World War, the life of the country had been transformed by defeat and occupation. The American presence was obvious everywhere. Apart from the political and other institutional changes which had been imposed by the victors, Japan was now looking to the United States as a mentor and model. Social habits, as I have already mentioned, had suffered many changes. Manners had become less formal. Women had begun to take a more active part in public life and were meeting together in societies for the pursuit of common interests.

Married women have always worked with their husbands and other members of their family in the small retail stores, workshops and farms, which until recently made up the greater part of the country's enterprise. Since the Second World War, however, large numbers of them have taken jobs in offices and factories, and they have been able to do this partly because of the changes that have taken place in the home. There have been modifications in the diet which have reduced the time spent by housewives in the preparation of meals. Many Japanese, for example, now eat a Western-style breakfast, with bread as its main constituent instead of rice. The introduction into the home of such appliances as refrigerators, cooking stoves using propane gas or electricity, washing machines and automatic rice-boilers has relieved the housewife of much tedious labour and has made it possible for her to go out to work.

The impact of American technology on Japanese industry was felt soon after the War, and the economic superiority of the United States confirmed her role as a model for Japanese manufacturers. After the Peace Treaty in 1952, there were reactions in some quarters against these influences and several of the political reforms introduced by the Occupation Authorities were modified. In the main, though, Japan realised that her political and economic interests required her to keep well within the American camp and the voice of dissent was subdued.

The fact that Britain after the Second World War had been obliged to leave responsibility for Japan almost entirely to the Americans was taken as a sign of her economic weakness. However, at the time of my visit in 1954, Japanese of the older generation had not fully accepted that British power was waning. The break-up of the British Empire, which was then in train, had not been widely appreciated. Some of my friends seemed to think that Britain's economic troubles were temporary and that before long she would again assert herself in the Far East. In 1954, the British played a prominent part in a Conference on Pacific Affairs held at Kyoto. A Japanese member of the diplomatic service whom I had known in England before the War asked me if the arrival in Japan of this group of Britons heralded a resumption of a positive British policy in the Far East. He was politely sceptical when I told him that in his part of the world our race was almost run.

Optimism concerning our economic and technological eminence also took some time to dissipate. In the early and mid-1950s Britain's reputation for high-quality products had not yet been tarnished. Her work in the development of jet aircraft and of radar showed that her technologists were competent and resourceful. The misfortunes of the Comet airliner at that time were commonly dismissed as teething troubles inevitable in pioneering ventures.

By the early 1960s the attitude was very different. Britain had joined the *Shayo-zoku* (tribes of the setting sun). She furnished the awful example of a stagnant economy, at the opposite pole from Japan, which had created the most rapidly expanding economy in the world. A few years later a favourite topic among economic journalists was the contrast between the performances of the two countries. Japanese businessmen, in general, had become pessimistic about Britain's future. Some of them contended that the British preference for an easy life and the breakdown of discipline in industrial relations were insurmountable obstacles to a sustained recovery. At the time of the devaluation of sterling in 1967, I asked a Japanese banker to give me his considered view of Britain's economic situation. After some hesitation he told me that he and his associates doubted whether devaluation would provide a lasting remedy for our troubles. He expected that Britain's economic weakness would continue and forecast that by the early 1970s the rate of exchange would have fallen to one dollar to the pound sterling.

When a friend who had been working in London for some years was recalled to a job in Japan, he told me that he would almost certainly find his new life disagreeable for a time, since he had become accustomed to British habits of work; now he had to adjust himself to the Japanese pace. I am not attempting here to analyse systematically the economic conditions of the two countries, but merely to present the opinions of Japanese friends and acquaintances about the British economy and to show how those opinions have changed over the years.

In recent visits to Japan I have often been asked by Japanese economists and civil servants whether I think that their country must at length inevitably succumb to the forces that have produced economic stagnation in Britain, itself once the most dynamic society in the world. Will success bring in its train a loss of energy and ambition? Will Japan ultimately be compelled to set up the whole elaborate apparatus of a Welfare State which, in the opinion of some Japanese, is a source of Britain's decline? I may add that even those who favour extensive social reforms and welfare measures modelled on those of Britain are inclined to think that the British practice of feather-bedding and of supporting failures has discouraged ambition and frustrated enterprise. Will it be possible, my friends ask, for their country to avoid following the awful example before her?

These are not easy questions to answer. Japan's rate of economic growth is likely to fall from its present exceptionally high level when she has completed the transference of her labour supply from relatively low-productivity work in agriculture and in small-scale industry and trade to the modern sector. In this respect she will be following the precedent set by Britain during the run-down of her agriculture in the nineteenth century. The rate of growth would also be affected if Japan were to cease concentrating her efforts on economic growth as the single or overriding national aim. This change is likely to show itself in a reduction in her present high rate of investment in manufacturing industry and in the application of more of her national income to consumption, social overhead capital and amenities, or to armaments and defence.

Some Japanese economists have come round to the view that a somewhat lower rate of growth would make it easier for their country to adapt itself to change. Others, half-seriously, have predicted the circumstances in which the pace is likely to be checked. They start from the proposition that the spirit of emulation has exerted a major influence in their country's achievements and argue that, in the absence of that spirit, energies might flag. As a friend put it to me: "Our economic growth is likely to continue only so long as there is some country ahead of us. When we have caught up with the United States we shall have no further incentive to advance."

My reflections on the diverse experience of Britain and Japan during the last thirty-five years have been prompted by discussions with Japanese friends and have led me to certain conclusions about the outstanding causes of the contrast. As I have already argued, Japan's success can be attributed to a fortunate convergence of various factors and to her possession of an institutional framework favourable to economic growth. Britain, though she still compares favourably with other countries as a civilised society, has for some decades been fretting in an institutional impasse. Traditional habits and ways of doing things which served her well in the past have become inappropriate to the circumstances of the twentieth century. Yet their very tenacity has impeded adaptation. I have sometimes thought that, in this respect, Britain could be compared with Imperial China during the last century of its existence when the government was said to have lost "the Mandate of Heaven". All the experience of China's leaders, even the skill and foresight of such men as Li Hung-Chang, was of no avail in the face of the conservatism of the great majority, whose conviction of China's innate superiority over all other nations was unshaken by the evidence of fact. Tradition or convention guided policy instead of a realistic appraisal of events. The government had lost the capacity to see things as they really were.

Even in the decades after the Revolution of 1911, China still seemed to be embedded in the past, whereas Japan was moving steadily into the new world. Yet beneath the surface great changes were being initiated. Dr Hu Shih, the Chinese Ambassador to the United States during the 1930s, made some percipient observations on these questions. He thought that the apparent contrast between China and Japan was misleading. He argued that while Japan had for years been advancing rapidly along the path of modernisation, she retained the institutions and social values of the past. In China, on the other hand, where the surface changes had been slight, the influence exerted by the outside world on the values of the old civilisation had been far more corrosive than in Japan. The next two decades did much to confirm his diagnosis. China was completely transformed by the Communist Revolution, whereas in Japan, even defeat, Occupation and an about-turn in policy left the foundations of her society intact. Since then, although Japan's institutions have been adapted to serve her policy of economic growth and although her outlook on the world has been modified, continuity with the past has not been broken. Hers has been a happier fate even though she first had to pass through much tribulation.

Analogies are of limited value in solving problems of this kind. This is certainly no place for speculating about how Britain will find her way out of her institutional impasse, or how and when Japan's rate of growth is likely to be moderated. Only the foolish would suppose that present trends will persist indefinitely. It is true that projections have lately been made on that assumption, and some of these actually purport to show the relative economic position of various countries (in terms of per capita gross national product) by the end of the century. All that needs to be said about these frivolous statistical exercises is that experience demonstrates conclusively that long-term economic forecasts are never fulfilled. In 1945 no one, not even the most optimistic among the Japanese themselves, imagined the heights that their country would scale by the 1960s. In thirty years' time it is probable that equally great changes in the world economy will have occurred and that these will have been attended by striking alterations in the relative economic position of different countries. We cannot at present have any notion of what they will be, but we may at least be sure that Clio's comments on current predictions will be no less ironical than usual simply because those predictions have passed through a computer.

Before leaving this topic, I should like to refer to my talk with a shrewd and perceptive Japanese economist who paid a visit to this country in 1957. He knew England well from previous visits, and on this occasion he was obviously perplexed and troubled by what he found. Manners, he thought, had deteriorated and a general slovenliness seemed to prevail. Had this something to do with the reaction of the British to their decline from the summits of world power? Was he witnessing the psychological as well as the economic consequences for Britain of the break-up of her Empire? I told him that the British people had not yet become fully conscious of what had happened and that many of them still deluded themselves into believing that the Commonwealth was merely the Empire writ large. Since that time, of course, their eyes have been opened, and I shall not debate whether, as my Japanese friend thought, the shock of acceptance has led to a paralysis of will. If this interpretation is true at all, it can apply only to the old and middle-aged. The young have always gone about their affairs heedless of the crumbling of empires. Nevertheless, it may be that the contraction of their horizons has robbed them of the assurance and panache of their forefathers.

Both Japan and Britain have lost their empires, although the circumstances in which the losses took place were very different. I have been impressed, however, with the contrasting attitudes of the Japanese and the British towards their imperialist past. The post-war Japanese have not allowed any regret for their former empire to temper the enthusiasm with which they have pursued new paths of ambition. Moreover, so far as I am aware, although their pre-war imperialism is discredited, most of them are not conscious of any shadow of guilt for their former ventures in colonialism, and they are puzzled at the contemporary attitude of Britain towards hers. Future historians may well consider that one of the oddest things about Britain's retreat from empire has been the efforts of many of her intellectual leaders to denigrate her former achievements. Japanese with whom I have talked on these matters find it difficult to understand why the present generation should feel guilty because its ancestors, whatever faults they committed, brought order and a measure of fair dealing to a large part of the globe, especially as these benefits have not everywhere survived the British withdrawal. I remember the incredulous amusement of Viscount Kato on learning, at the Pacific Relations Conference in 1954, that the expansion in their armaments by India and Pakistan was being directed not against an external aggressor but against each other. It may be that educated Japanese, having a strong historical sense, do not easily fall into the error of judging the conduct of men of past times by the standards that happen to be fashionable today. Or the explanation may simply be that the present generation denies any identity with the imperialists of the past.

I must not end this sketch of opinion about Britain and the British without referring to more favourable judgements. Many Japanese who know the world find Britain

Appointment in Japan

one of the most agreeable countries to live in. Our towns seem quiet and uncongested compared with Tokyo and Osaka. Even those who look askance at our sorry economic performance find in Britain amenities that are lacking at home. They admire our parks, our gardens and country estates. A Japanese banker with experience of many cities told me that he thought London was the world's most civilised capital. Such favourable opinions are probably more usual now than they were a few years ago, for evidence of the disagreeable social and ecological results of very rapid growth have been accumulating in Japan and, as I have shown, criticism of growth as a goal of policy is mounting. "The reason we work so hard," said a Japanese friend, wryly, "is because we are so much more comfortable in our offices and factories than we are at home." No doubt the lavish fringe benefits and welfare facilities now provided at places of work by most of the large firms serve to sharpen this contrast. Another friend, after experience abroad as a student, had been reflecting on British and Japanese ways of living. He had reached the conclusion that we lived more sensibly than his countrymen and that we made adequate provision for leisure and entertainment. His own father and many of his father's generation, he added, had spent all their waking moments at work and had had little pleasure out of life.

This attitude, though almost certainly not typical, is symptomatic of an emerging spirit of social criticism. Japan could not have achieved her great successes without the sustained and devoted efforts of workers and staff at all levels. The resourceful self-made pioneers, such as Honda and Matsushita, whose genius has built up massive new industries, and the shrewd policy-makers in the bureaucracy, could not have accomplished so much if they had not been able to call on the disciplined millions. For many of these, especially for men in the managerial or administrative grades in business, the professions or the Civil Service, life has taken on a strict pattern to which they have to conform. When they start their careers they know within rather narrow limits the timing of each step ahead, provided that their own energies do not flag. There is an almost inevitable progression up the ladder of a career from competitive success in school and university, through the various stages of responsibility, to retirement at the age of fifty-five or so.

Some Japanese have become restive under this weight of uniformity, and the limitations that such a life imposes have provided a popular theme for contemporary satirists. I shall not venture to speculate on the generality of this resentment nor the bitterness of the criticism. The feelings may not go very deep. The rise in the real incomes of nearly all employees, particularly in the modern sector of the economy, has been so rapid and so substantial that it would be surprising indeed if most of them were not more conscious of the benefits of economic expansion than of its pains. Nevertheless, the time may be approaching when the Japanese will cease to find the single-minded pursuit of economic growth satisfying and when their authorities will have to draw on all their wealth of experience and social tact in reshaping the country's policies.

* * * * *

I must not end this book in the antechambers of political and economic debate, nor even on their threshold. This is a book of reminiscences, and although I have been a student of Japan's economic affairs for sixty years, on this occasion I am only incidentally concerned with them. Here I have tried to recall my delight in the Japanese scene and in personal relations. These are the gifts from Japan that I have valued most. I congratulate myself that I was fortunate in the timing of my first acquaintance with the country. It is perhaps rash for anyone who must admit the sharp reproach of years to commit himself to any opinion of how present-day Japan appears to a young Englishman on his first visit. He will certainly have much to admire in practical achievement. Yet I cannot believe that he is now able to find his way into the magical world into which I was admitted sixty years ago. In 1922 Japan still breathed the air of her feudal past. The beauty of the countryside had few blemishes. Modern technology and Western influences had not yet shattered the fabric of traditional life. As I went about my everyday business, it seemed to me that I was being presented with glimpses, now of the ancient world, now of the mediaeval world, and now of a world beyond the imagination of an untravelled European at any time in history.

E. M. Forster once said that the reading and re-reading of a great novel made him "realise how many ways there are of being alive". To live in a country with an entirely different civilisation from one's own brings the same realisation. Japan offered me, at an early age, the opportunity to share in her ways of living. From the first, I was an appreciative guest at the feast she provided and my gratitude for her hospitality has not grown less with the passing of the years.

Glossary

Japanese words used in the text are listed below.

Amerikajin	American
Amado	wooden sliding screen or shutter
Baka	fool
Banto	company executive
Benjo	lavatory
Besso	large villa
Bonsai	dwarf trees
Chosenjin	Korean
Dai Ichi Koto Gakko	First Higher School
Dai Hachi Kkoto Gakko	Eighth Higher School
Dai Nihon	Great Japan
Daikon	large radish
Daimyo	Lord
Dan	decision, step
Dan-dan to	gradually
Danshaku	Baron
Departo	department store
Edokko	native of downtown Tokyo
Eta	outcast
Furoshiki	squares of cloth used for tying up possessions
Fusaumå	sliding screen door

Appointment in Japan

Futon	mattress
Gautama	Buddha
Geji-geji	large centipede
Genkan	entrance hall
Genro	elder statesman
Geta	wooden clogs
Ginbura	evening stroll along the Ginza, Tokyo's main shopping street
Giri	obligation, duty
Happi	labourer's cotton tunic
Hibachi	firebox
Heimin	commoners
Iwa	rock
Jin-rikisha	one-man rickshaw
Jishin	earthquake
Junsen-ji keizai	quasi-wartime economy
Kami	Shinto deities
Kamuso	basket-like straw hats
Kanai	one's own wife
Kanji	Chinese characters
Karakasa	adjustable paper umbrella
Katakana	one of the two Japanese syllabaries
Kendo	fencing
Kiku-ningyo	puppet performances
Kotatsu	charcoal stove sunk in the floor
Koto	stringed instrument that rests on the floor
Koto Gakko	High School
Koto Gogyo Gakko	Technical High School
Koto Shogyo Gakko	Commercial High School
Kusai	smelly
Mino	straw cape

Glossary

Mizuho-no-kuni	The Land of Fresh Rice Ears, ancient name for Japan
Mobo	modern boy
Moga	modern girl
Nagauta	ballad
Nashi	Japanese pear
Nori	dried seaweed, or paste, starch
Nikai	upper storey of a house
Noh	Japanese drama with dance and song
Obi	sash or belt
O-bon	Festival of the Dead
Okusan	another person's wife
O-soji	house cleaning
Pan	bread
Ringisei	system of business management by which consensus is reached by consultation with all levels of employees
Romaji	Roman letters
Ronin	masterless Samurai
Sake	Japanese rice wine
Samurai	member of military class, warrior
Seiyojin	Westerner
Semi	cicada
Sen	coin, one-hundredth of a yen
Sensei	teacher
Seto-mono	pottery
Shakuhachi	flute
Shamisen	musical instrument
Shibui	preference for unostentatious or even austere beauty
Shikataganai	expression of inevitability
Shinajin	Chinese

Shin-cha	green tea plucked first in the year, new tea
Shizoku	descendants of the Samurai
Shogun	General
Shoji	sliding screens
Soroban	abacus
Suiheisha	society of declassed people, official term for outcasts
Sukiyaki	typical Japanese dish
Sumo	Japanese wrestling
Tabi	Japanese-style socks
Tatami	reed-covered straw mat
Tempura	Japanese dish
Tokonoma	alcove in which is displayed painting, pot, flower arrangement etc. Focal point of a reception room
Tojin Okichi	foreigner (Okich – "of the foreigners")
Uchiwa	round fan
Yamato	ancient name for Japan
Yubi	fingers or toes
Yukata	unlined cotton kimono worn in summer
Zaibatsu	business houses
Zen	sect of Buddhism, religious meditation
Zori	straw footwear

Index

Adams, Will, 15
American influence, 70, 75, 86, 139, 173, 180–2
Ashley, C. A., 154
Ashley, W. J., 1–2, 117–8

Birmingham University, 1, 117
Blacker, Carmen, 166
Blunden, Edmund, 114
British Empire, 175–80, 182, 186–7; relations with Japan, 179–80, 182–4, 186–8

Chamberlain, Basil, 11–2
changes, 5, 41–5, 85–7, 90, 126–7, 168–71, 180–1
China, 55, 154–7, 166–8, 172–3, 180, 185
Claudel, Paul, 150
colleagues and friends, 9, 64, 66–7, 69, 92, 124, 137–44, 152
customs and attitudes: collective tradition, 82–3; hierarchy 99–103; obligation, 103–6, 111–2; restraint, 84–6

Dan, Baron Takuma, 117–8
dress, 6, 27, 38, 40, 41–4

Earthquake of 1923, 120–7
economic growth, 158–84; comparison with GB, 182–7; costs of, 165–9, 188
education, 70–7
Erasmus, image of, 89–90

food, 7, 21–2, 116, 146–8, 181
Fukusuke Tabi Company, 108

Geisha, 23, 31, 37, 50, 95, 111–2, 139, 141, 143–6; Gion *geisha*, 144, 146; Shimbashi *geisha*, 51
Genroku period, 26

Hara, Prime Minister, 62
Harris, Townsend, 95
Hearn, Lafcadio, 24, 114
Hiroshige, 32
Hitotsubashi University (formerly Tokyo University of Commerce), 1, 57, 73
Honda, 188
houses, description of, 16–20, 24–8, 126–7

Immigration Act, US, 54–6, 128, 178
Imperial Rescript on Education, 107
industry, 34–6, 40–1, 131–3, 158–64
Inouye, Professor, 3
Ise, 21, 29–30
Ishibashi, Tanzan, 46, 130
Iwata, Mrs (housekeeper), 20–5, 26, 27, 178

Japanese Federation of Industries, 132

Kabuki theatre, 42, 51, 113, 140–1, 148
Kato, Viscount, 117, 187
Kegon Falls, 111, 151
Keio University, 72, 76
Kikugoro, 140
Kobe, 3, 166, 177
Komeito, the, 172
Kyoto, 9, 40–1, 42, 118, 125, 146, 154, 182

language, puns and solecisms, 10–4, 65, 117–8

Marubeni, 40
Marxist economics, 66–7
Matsumura, Takeshi, 15
Matsushita, 188
Meiji period, 6, 39, 55, 72, 78, 80–1
Mikimoto, 106, 148
militarism, rise of, 128–33, 173
Minobe, Professor, 81
Mitsubishi, 35, 64, 72
Mitsui, 1, 7, 117, 129, 131, 179
Mizuho-cho, 16–20, 31–2, 49

Nagoya: countryside, 46–9; industry, 34–6; physical description, 5–6, 34, 36–9, 45–9
Nagoya *Koto Shogyo Gakko*, 1, 57–65, 67–71, 99
Nicholls, A. E., 6, 16
Noh plays, 141–2
Noritake (Nippon Toki), 34–5

Ohira, Prime Minister, 84
oratorial contests, 67–9
Osaka, 39, 120, 130, 188

Pacific Relations Conference 1954, 182, 187
prices, 32–3, 43, 161

Raucat, Thomas, 90
religion, rituals and superstition, 19, 24, 27–8, 39, 49–51, 80, 105–110

Sansom, Sir George, 78, 104–5, 114, 132
Snellen, J. B., 89
Soka Gakkai, the, 172
Sopwiths, 35
students, 30, 57–63, 67–70, 138, 149
Suzuki, Kenkichi, 14–5

Takamori, Saigo, 117
Terauchi, General, 117
Tokai Bank, 8
Tokugawa period, 45
Tokyo, 51, 89, 122–6, 145, 165, 177, 188

Waseda University, 61
Watanabe, Dr R., 8–9, 105, 143
women, 33, 85–6, 114, 159, 174, 181

Yokohama, 122, 123, 125, 177
Yokohama Specie Bank, 176
Young, Morgan, 133–5